CREATING QUILTS WITH SIMPLE SHAPES

Ann Castleberry
and Mischele Hart

Martingale™
& COMPANY

Creating Quilts with Simple Shapes
Ann Castleberry and Mischele Hart
© 2001 by Ann Castleberry and Mischele Hart

Martingale & Company
20205 144th Ave. NE
Woodinville, WA 98072-8478
www.martingale-pub.com

Printed in China
06 05 04 03 02 01   8 7 6 5 4 3 2 1

Library of Congress Cataloging-in-Publication Data

Castleberry, Ann
    Creating quilts with simple shapes / Ann Castleberry and Mischele Hart.
        p. cm.
    ISBN 1-56477-371-X
    1. Quilts—Design. 2. Color in textile crafts.
    3. Patchwork—Patterns. I. Hart, Mischele. II. Title.

TT835 .C392 2001   2001022255
746.46'041—dc21

Mission Statement

We are dedicated to providing quality products and service by working together to inspire creativity and to enrich the lives we touch.

CREDITS

President ∾ Nancy J. Martin
CEO ∾ Daniel J. Martin
Publisher ∾ Jane Hamada
Editorial Director ∾ Mary V. Green
Editorial Project Manger ∾ Tina Cook
Technical Editor ∾ Jane Townswick
Copy Editor ∾ Karen Koll
Design and Production Manager ∾ Stan Green
Illustrator ∾ Robin Strobel
Cover ∾ Rohani Design
Text Designer ∾ Rohani Design
Photographer ∾ Brent Kane

Dedication

To our parents, Jack and Dorothy Castleberry and Claude and Nora Jackson, for teaching us that we could do whatever we wanted as long as we could imagine it.

To our children, Brian Hart, Leighton and Mary Craig Hart, and Christopher Svastits, for bringing more joy to our lives than we could have imagined and teaching us that the simplest of things have the greatest possibilities.

To our husbands, Donald Hart and Edmund Svastits, for inspiring us to imagine what neither of us could have done alone.

Acknowledgments

Our wholehearted thanks to the following people:

Mary Ellen Hopkins, who originally taught us to open our eyes and minds to the concept that the design possibilities are endless for the most basic of blocks

Jackie Robinson, for encouraging us throughout the entire process and then quilting "Turquoise Tango" for us

Our many quilting friends who supported us by piecing and quilting projects for us, including Cathy Leitner, ruthie miller, Sandy Pozetta, Jackie Robinson, Sandra Sontag, Carol Stanley, Shirley Swanson, Adrienne Tavares, and Becky Valcante

A very special group of teachers and quilt-shop owners who are always ready to sew when we get the "itch," including Suzan Drury, Sandy Heminger, Mary Huey, Jean Humenansky, Jan Kreuger, Jackie Robinson, and Jill Wyman

Adrienne Taveres, Mischele's business partner of many years, for being a friend and for providing the quiet, unfailing, and constant support that has allowed Mischele to teach, design, and write

Marcie and Herb Kelly, our favorite baby-sitters, for taking care of our beloved little dude, Christopher, and always acting like we are doing you a favor for bringing him to visit you

Karen Thrush, for taking the wonderful "About the Authors" photograph that manages to make us both look glamorous, as well as many photos of our favorite little dude

Nancy J. Martin and the entire staff of Martingale & Company, for believing in two beginning writers and cheerfully responding to all of our seemingly endless questions

Each other, for having way too much fun designing all the many projects and then finishing everything in time for the deadline (while still remaining friends!)

Contents

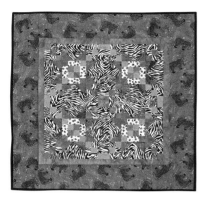

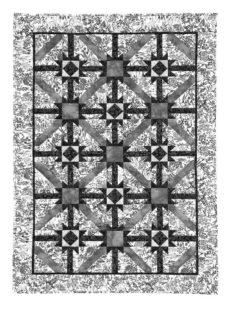

Foreword

One of the principal themes of my book *The It's Okay If You Sit on My Quilt Book* and its subsequent series is that any quilter can make an unlimited number of fresh and unique quilt designs using just one or two pieced blocks. For example, all the quilts included in *Baker's Dozen Doubled* are made with the classic Four Patch and Nine Patch blocks. I am so glad to see two of my favorite and very prolific students, Ann Castleberry and Mischele Hart, build on this basic idea in *Creating Quilts with Simple Shapes.*

Rather than simply writing another project book, Ann and Mischele have developed a systematic process for creating original quilt designs using easy-to-piece shapes. As in my It's Okay series, all the quilts in this book can be made using squares, rectangles, half-square triangles, and plain blocks, some of which incorporate the widely published connector concepts that I developed. Using these classic, simple-to-sew shapes means that quilters at all levels of experience will be able to focus on creating fresh, progressive designs rather than on mastering sewing skills.

Two of the most frequent comments I hear as I travel and teach around the world are "Where should I start in choosing fabric for this project?" and "I want to use this specific fabric in my next project—where do I begin?" Chapter 3 of this book answers those questions using the authors' approach of developing a fabric theme that corresponds to the primary design theme. Quilters, regardless of their experience, are always looking for a surefire way of selecting the right fabrics to enhance every project. The flow-chart in chapter 3 is a great starting point.

Ann and Mischele present four design progressions in *Creating Quilts with Simple Shapes.* No two of the quilts look alike. Each design is fresh and unique, without being difficult or time-consuming to create. These two students "got" what I've been saying for years, and they have expanded on it. It's very flattering for me, as a teacher, mentor, and friend, to see that the seeds I've sown are sprouting so nicely. The processes in this book really do make it possible to create a quilt for each of the loved ones in your life, so with my blessings, get ready for great new creative adventures.

Mary Ellen Hopkins

Introduction

Have you ever been inspired to make a quilt for someone you love, yet been unable to find exactly the right pattern that would express the emotion or idea you want to convey? Or have you seen a pattern in a book and thought, "I really like that basic idea, but what I want to do is use this great new bug fabric in a quilt for my nephew who's going off to study biology at the university"? In either of these situations, you're stuck with spending time looking for the right pattern or with modifying a pattern you already have so that you can finish the quilt quickly and easily.

As children and teenagers, we all wanted to be special and unique. Yet as adults, we sometimes fail to appreciate our wonderful qualities. Designing a quilt is a great way to express your individuality, and it's a tangible reminder of the truly imaginative person within you. However, designing a quilt can cause even the most experienced quilter to feel insecure.

The term *design* is often bandied about during discussions about quiltmaking. The word has several connotations, depending upon the context in which it is being used.

In this book, we use the word *design* to refer to the effect that you want to create in a pieced quilt. You might want to make a quilt that depicts a starry night sky or use heart fabrics and shapes to express love for a special person in your life. You can convey these things in your quilt's design.

Our unique design approach using simple shapes reduces insecurities and gives you a framework for success. Once you feel comfortable with the process, you'll be able to concentrate on increasing or enhancing the visual interest of each quilt you make. These are our goals in writing this book:

- To provide a structured, easy-to-follow approach to creating quilt designs using simple shapes
- To present design concepts in an approachable manner, so that no matter what your level of quilting experience, you will feel secure in creating new quilt designs
- To introduce the concept of individual block construction, so that you can design quilts as you go along, experimenting on a design wall, rather than having to plan out an entire project before you start
- To provide quilt projects that you can use as jumping-off points for developing your own quilt designs

Chapter 1 discusses using basic, simple shapes to create quilt designs. This allows you to concentrate on the design process itself, rather than on quilt construction.

In chapter 2, we present our step-by-step process for designing an original quilt. We divide each principal step into easy-to-accomplish activities, with corresponding examples.

Chapter 3 features a similar step-by-step process for choosing fabrics for a quilt design.

In chapters 4 and 5, we offer a variety of design ideas, progressions, and concrete examples and projects.

Chapter 6 contains the pep talk we like to include in our workshop: "Why not try creating your next project—you may actually enjoy it!"

Chapter 7 contains the basic techniques you will need for making the fourteen quilts in this book. You can use the project instructions to make great quilts or as starting points for your own original and dazzling designs.

We hope you will have as much fun using simple shapes as we have had writing this book.

Ann Castleberry and Mischele Hart

1

Simple Shapes
and Simple Variations

Mary Ellen Hopkins revolutionized quilting when she wrote *The It's Okay If You Sit on My Quilt Book*. The focus of her book (and the now-classic series based on ideas in it) is that simple pieced shapes can be used to create complex, visually interesting quilt designs. Mary Ellen's long career and the popularity of her books have shown that it is virtually impossible to exhaust the design potential of simple shapes in creating quilts based either on one shape or on combinations of several shapes. For example, it is possible to spend ten years making quilts based solely on half-square triangles without ever repeating the same design or running out of ideas. Here are some traditional, commonly

used shapes in quiltmaking and the blocks we use in this book that are based on these shapes.

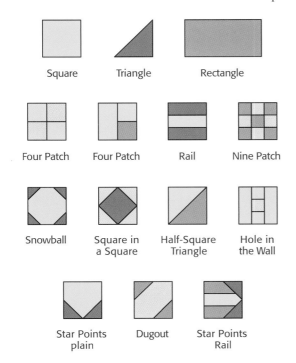

Some simple shapes result from altering a basic property of the original shape, changing the proportions of shapes within a block, erasing lines in a block, or sewing together two shapes to create a different shape. One familiar quiltmaking shape that comes from sewing together two Half-Square Triangle blocks is the Flying Goose. An even simpler way to construct this Flying Goose shape would be to sew two

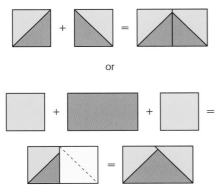

Two Half-Square Triangle blocks or two connector squares and one rectangle create one Flying Goose shape.

plain squares to a single rectangle. Plain squares that are used in this way to create triangle shapes are called "connector" squares. See page 58 for detailed directions on using connector squares.

Sewing two Half-Square Triangle blocks together can also create a Pinwheel shape. Another way to achieve this same effect would be to sew two plain squares onto opposing corners of a rectangle. (See page 58 for directions on using connector squares.)

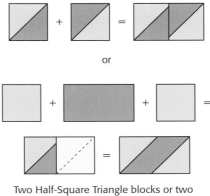

Two Half-Square Triangle blocks or two connector squares and one rectangle create one Pinwheel shape.

Focusing on Squares and Rectangles

For simplicity, we used only square and rectangle blocks to create the quilts presented in this book. The advantages to using these simple shapes for designing quilts include the following:

- You can use either graph paper or a computerized quilting-design program to develop your ideas.
- You can focus your energy on creating exciting quilt designs and variations instead of on learning special sewing skills or complicated techniques.
- You can feature today's fabrics, rather than complicated shapes, in your quilts.

chapter 2
A Systematic Approach to Design

Very rarely does a complex quilt design emerge complete in your mind; rather, it is usually the product of working through a systematic design process. We have mapped out our systematic approach to designing a quilt on a flowchart that is easy to work through. You can spend a few minutes or a few hours at each stage, depending upon the complexity you desire in your quilt design. Our flowchart consists of three major phases, each of which is discussed in greater detail in the following pages.

Creating a primary design

↓

Creating secondary designs

↓

Finalizing a design

four steps on this flowchart show our systematic approach to creating a primary quilt design. Primary design is the first aspect you notice when looking at a quilt. A detailed discussion of each step follows.

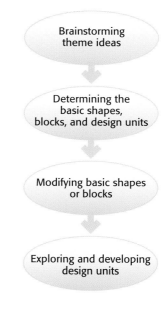

Brainstorming theme ideas

↓

Determining the basic shapes, blocks, and design units

↓

Modifying basic shapes or blocks

↓

Exploring and developing design units

Note: In this book, a design unit is a pattern created by the juxtaposition of blocks in a quilt top. When you are planning your quilt design you will sew sample design units to aid in the design process. When assembling a quilt top, however, you never sew design units ahead of time. You always work with loose blocks. See "Assembling a Quilt Top with the Four-Patch Method" on page 62.

Creating a Primary Design

The primary design of a quilt can be shown in a line drawing that indicates the seams of the quilt. It also carries an emotional aspect, or mood. The

Brainstorming Theme Ideas

Brainstorming is a fun and easy technique for developing a new idea. The ground rule is that during a brainstorming session, all ideas, whether practical or ludicrous, must be entertained. No suggestions can be rejected initially, because any suggestion has potential. You can create a theme for a quilt by listing some or all of the following:

- Intended recipient of or reason for the quilt (for example, a nephew who is graduating from high school or a holiday celebration)
- Basic subject matter of the quilt (such as stars, tropical flowers, or cats)
- Fundamental shapes or blocks or design units you want to use in the quilt (for example, star shapes for a celestial theme or Rail blocks to portray stripes on a flag)

Tip Every time you attempt to create a quilt design, you learn something useful. It isn't necessary to use every idea in your next quilt project.

Let's use the example of making a quilt for a nephew who is graduating from high school and going off to college to study bugs (entomology). Your brainstorming session might result in a list like this one, which you can use for developing your primary design.

- Nephew's favorite color is blue; he likes optical illusions
- Bugs: bug fabric, bugs live outside
- Can't think of a shape that screams "bug" to me, but I have a great bug fabric that I don't want to cut into small pieces—want to be able to see more of the bugs in the finished quilt
- I only have time to make a wall hanging for his new dorm room, not a bed quilt (wall hangings also easier to quilt and less likely to be abused)

Tip The trick to avoiding frustration during a personal brainstorming session is to know when to put the paper and pencil away. Remember—world peace does not depend on you creating the perfect quilt design in fifteen minutes.

The list from your brainstorming session might help you make decisions, such as, "I want to make a small quilt highlighting the piece of great bug fabric in my stash. I also have some optical-illusion black-and-white stripe fabrics that would go well with it. And I saw a gross-but-wonderful, yellow-green fabric at the quilt shop that reminded me of squished bugs—better take a break and go buy some of that before it is gone." When you have reached this point, you are ready to decide on the basic shapes, blocks, and design units you want to use in your quilt.

Determining the Basic Shapes, Blocks, and Design Units

Some design themes naturally suggest certain shapes, blocks, or design units. For example, Sawtooth Star and Rail blocks would be appropriate for a quilt with a patriotic theme. Many other themes, however, are not associated with specific shapes, blocks, or design units. For example, a baby's first-birthday quilt would not automatically suggest particular shapes, blocks, or design units. And a bug quilt for a nephew's graduation would not immediately bring to mind shapes that represent bugs (let alone all those legs that bugs have!). Ask yourself the following questions when you are deciding which basic shapes, blocks, and design units you want to include in your quilt design:

- How much time do I have available for making this quilt? Some blocks can be sewn together more quickly than others. For example, it is faster to make strip sets for Rail blocks than to make the same number of Snowball blocks, which are not made with strip sets.

- How large an area of each fabric do I want to show in the quilt design? If you want to highlight a certain fabric, you might decide to make blocks that contain larger plain areas. For example, the center area of a Snowball block would be a good place to show off a dynamite floral print.

- What will the finished dimensions of the quilt be? Some blocks adapt better than others to size limitations. For example, it can be challenging to stitch 1½" finished Snowball blocks, while 1½" finished Four Patch blocks are easy and quick to make.

Modifying Basic Shapes or Blocks

At this early stage, you can modify basic shapes or blocks easily if you wish. Changing the size of a shape or playing with proportions in a block will add your own personal flair to a quilt design, and it might suggest an exciting avenue to explore in future quilts. Making changes to traditional proportions can emphasize a shape within a block; for example, changing from equal-size rectangles to narrow-wide-narrow rectangles in a Rail block will cause the largest rail to be the most prominent shape in the block. Here is a way to explore making changes to basic shapes or blocks:

1. Do a line drawing of any basic block you would like to work with, using either a pencil and graph paper or a computerized drafting program.
2. Do a second line drawing of the same block, this time changing the proportion of one or more of the shapes in it.
3. Using colored pencils, color in the altered shapes. Evaluate the effect of the changes.

4. Make multiple photocopies of your changed blocks, so that you can arrange them in different configurations.

Here is an example of changing the proportion of shapes in the traditional Pinwheel block. By making one of the two triangle shapes smaller and sewing two of the changed blocks together we created our unique Tampa block.

Pinwheel block   Tampa block

Exploring and Developing Design Units

Cut out your photocopied blocks and arrange them in various combinations on a piece of white paper. Use temporary adhesive to hold the blocks in place. Explore different possibilities until you create a design unit that pleases you. Then tape the blocks on the paper in that arrangement. This example shows a Tampa block at left, along with a Tampa design unit at right. The unit contains four Tampa blocks (A), a center Square in a Square block (B), and plain blocks in the corners (C).

Tampa block

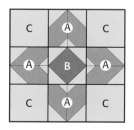

Tampa design unit

Creating Secondary Designs

Creating secondary designs involves the four steps shown on this flowchart. Each of these steps begins with the word *exploring,* because you need to consider each idea, experiment by trying out a few alternatives, and then determine which choices are appropriate for your quilt.

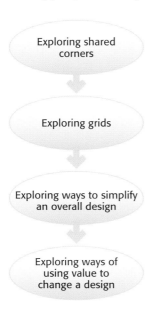

Exploring Shared Corners

The term "shared corners" means that two neighboring design units share the same block at their corners, a concept pioneered by Mary Ellen Hopkins. To see how shared corners work,

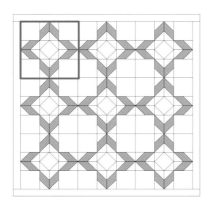

Traditional Puss in the Corner design

start by taking a look at the way Puss in the Corner design units look when they are placed side by side without any overlap or sharing of corner blocks (below left). This is a pleasing design, but it has limited design possibilities.

By moving the Puss in the Corner design units so they share neighboring plain corner blocks, we changed the design. The design units now look like they are set diagonally, which creates more interesting patterns and offers greater possibilities for introducing secondary design elements. Sharing corners works most effectively with design units that have a common corner-block shape (such as a plain or Four Patch block).

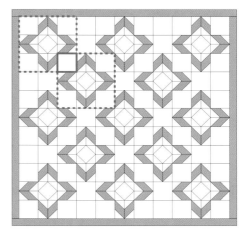

Puss in the Corner design with shared corner blocks

Exploring Grids

Grids are the secondary design elements you can create with sashing strips or plain areas of a quilt design. Typically, we think of sashing strips as narrow areas that visually separate more important design units in a quilt design. Traditional sashing strips often feature small corner squares at the intersections. However, by adding additional shapes to them you can make sashing strips just as important as the design units themselves. This creates even more potential for developing interesting secondary designs.

This quilt shows how you can create intricate, complex designs by making simple changes to the sashing strips. We added Star Points Rail blocks to the sashing strips between the smaller blocks, adding zip to the simple overall quilt design. See "Bugs!" on page 88.

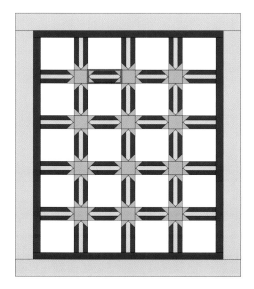

You can also create grids by introducing shapes into plain blocks in design units. The quilt below features Tampa design units that share corners. The overall quilt design has a diagonal feel. You can add a secondary grid to this overall design by replacing the plain blocks with Dugout blocks. See "Tampas Go Hawaiian" on page 84.

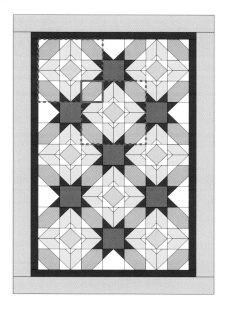

Exploring Ways to Simplify an Overall Design

You can change and simplify the appearance of an overall quilt design by eliminating lines or shapes within a block or blocks. In this design, for example, there are twelve Four Patch Star design units arranged in four rows of three design units each.

Original design

Eliminating lines in the outer rectangles along the edges of the design makes the stars appear to float on the background. This simplifies the overall design and focuses the viewer's attention on the primary design in the center of the quilt.

Simplified design

Exploring Ways of Using Value to Change a Design

Value is the relative lightness or darkness of a fabric. The value of a fabric depends on the value of the fabrics that surround it. You can vary values to emphasize individual blocks or design units. For a more complete discussion of value, see "Using Value Effectively" on page 24.

The three quilts pictured below, each featuring the same basic Puss in the Corner design

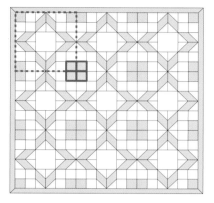

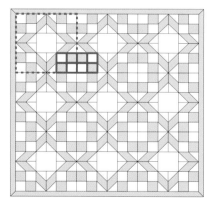

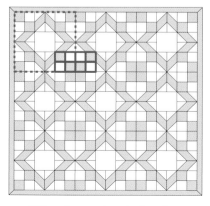

Different secondary designs from Puss in the Corner units.

units, show how value can create secondary designs. In the first quilt, the Four Patch corner blocks are all dark. The middle quilt shows alternating darks and lights in the Four Patch blocks, and in the third quilt, the lights and darks in the Four Patch blocks are rotated 90°.

Finalizing a Design

Your quilt design should be coming together nicely at this point. You have already made most of your design decisions, and there are only a few more choices to tackle. We encourage you to take time at this point to sew together samples of each different type of block you plan to use in your quilt design and sew the blocks into design units. Remember, this is the only time you will sew blocks into design units; in quilt-top construction, you will sew blocks together with our four-patch construction system (see page 62). When you select fabrics for samples, pay more attention to the value of each fabric than to the color or print. The most important thing is accurate placement of values within your samples. You can easily substitute a dark red for a dark blue when you finalize your fabric selections for the quilt. After you finish making your samples, do any or all of the following:

- Arrange your sample design units on a design wall and stand back to evaluate your results.

Tip Try viewing sample design units through an empty paper-towel tube (toilet-paper tubes are too short). The long tube will focus your eye on the areas of interest on the design wall and eliminate visual distractions. You'll be able to spot areas needing correction immediately.

- Place your design units on a table and place a folding mirror next to them to create multiples of them visually. Then evaluate your results.
- If you like working on a computer and own a scanner, scan your design units and create an "electronic quilt" using computer image-manipulation software.

When you view your sewn samples, you may find that something seems wrong but you have no idea what the problem is. This can happen when you have been working intensely on a design idea, selecting fabrics, or facing a deadline. If you find yourself unable to analyze or identify what is bothering you about your samples or design, try the following:

- Ask a member of your family for an opinion and suggestions. Often, people who don't know anything about design or fabric can immediately spot the problem area and offer good solutions.
- Ask a quilting friend for opinions (at the least, you'll get sympathy and comfort).
- Leave the samples on the design wall for a few days and view them again—you'll see them with fresh eyes and renewed enthusiasm, and new ideas may pop into your head right away.
- Think through your design process and reconsider the choices you made at each stage. Often, changing the results of just one step can get your project back on target.

Chapter 3

Selecting Fabrics and Colors

After you have finalized your quilt design, it's time to select the fabrics you want to use in your quilt. We've never met a quilter who wasn't insecure about choosing fabrics and colors. Everyone wishes there could be a single, simple rule that applied to all quilts. Choosing fabric for a specific project can be more stressful than creating a design. After all, the materials used for designing are relatively inexpensive—some paper and a few pencils or a computer quilt-design program. But fabric is expensive and can be irreplaceable. The information in this chapter will give you more confidence in your fabric-selection process. Pay special attention to the information in "Using Value Effectively" on page 24.

Read through the following guidelines, and then choose colors and fabrics that will enhance the design and make your finished quilt a show-stopper.

Reproducing a Sample

There are good reasons for making a quilt that is like one you've already seen and admired—you know that you already like the fabrics, and you're sure you will be happy with the finished product. Unfortunately, it is usually unrealistic to expect to be able to make a quilt that is exactly like one that is already finished. More often than not, sample quilts were made long before you ever saw them. We sometimes use samples for our workshops and classes for several years. And making a quilt that looks just like a sample quilt will not give you the opportunity to expand your quilting horizons and grow as a creative quilter.

Fabric manufacturers typically introduce new lines of fabric two or three times per year. Each new line can include as many as ten to twelve prints, in four or five colorways *each*, for a minimum of forty to fifty fabrics per line. That means that many companies offer upwards of one hundred fabrics in a year's time—and who has the storage space to collect a piece of every fabric available on the market? You can easily substitute fabrics you already own for fabrics in a sample quilt you like, using what we call the "representative of" rule. Think of your stash as a fabric palette and make purchases accordingly.

The "Representative of" Rule

Think of each fabric in a quilt as being characteristic or representative of a certain type of fabric. For example, one large-scale floral print can be substituted for another, one tone-on-tone fabric can take the place of another, and one novelty or conversation print will often work for another. So although you may not be able to make your project identical to a sample you have seen and liked, you can still make it look very similar by following these steps:

- Take a close look at the sample quilt and evaluate the different types of fabric in it (for example, a geometric print with three colors, a pastel tone-on-tone fabric, and so on).

- Determine the theme fabric used in the sample quilt.
- Determine the lesser and background fabrics in the sample.
- Determine the relative value of each fabric in the sample quilt, ranging from darkest to lightest. (For example, the darkest value might be the theme fabric, the next darkest value a dominant fabric, the lesser fabrics mediums, and the background fabric the lightest value.)
- Choose your fabrics based on their relative values, not their colors. This will enable you to choose fabrics that will create a similar, yet not identical, look.

Buying to Enhance Your Fabric Palette

After buying fabric for several years, most quilters have built up an impressive stash. We have never conducted a workshop where someone has not asked for our opinions on how much of any fabric to buy for a personal fabric palette. There are no magic answers to this question—solutions depend upon the contents of your current collection, your available finances and storage space, your desire to own more fabric, and the tolerance level of your spouse or roommate. However, we do provide these general guidelines for making systematic fabric purchases that will enhance and expand your fabric palette.

- Take an inventory of your current stash. Ideally you should have a light, medium, and dark value of each of the twelve colors on the color wheel, as well as an assortment of neutrals (white, gray, tan, black). Focus your future purchases on filling in any gaps you discover. For example, we are currently looking for interesting multicolored background fabrics and light reds that are not pink or orange.

- Don't replace the fabric you used in the project you just finished; look for new fabric lines and colors.
- Remember that the fabric market is like the fashion market—what's "in" today may be "out" tomorrow. For example, dusty, grayed tones were very popular in the early 90s, while clearer, brighter colors are more popular now. Often, older fabrics make great "back-of-the-quilt" art.
- Remember that most novelty fabrics are cute, fun, and interchangeable. Try to limit your purchases of novelty fabric unless you have a specific project in mind.
- Make it a habit to purchase a yard of a new color and play around with it. We rarely buy less than a yard of anything, because we make lots of test pieces and enjoy using colors in unexpected ways.
- Consider buying at least three yards of a fabric that appears to be a good theme or background fabric. This amount is usually enough for blocks, border, and binding.
- Think about buying a whole bolt (ten to fifteen yards) of an absolutely terrific theme or background fabric that you know you will use a lot of. We typically buy an entire bolt when we fall in love with a fabric because we often make a series of projects, samples, or quilts based on a few key fabrics. Your local quilt shop may give you a discount if you purchase an entire bolt. However, don't just park the bolt in the closet and wait for inspiration. *Use it!*
- Start a collection of light-value fabrics. Without looking at your stash, we can guess that you have few light fabrics. Until recently, there were not many lighter fabrics available that weren't either very plain (white or tan background prints) or sky or cloud prints. Recently, however, fabric manufacturers have started to introduce marvelous lighter-value fabrics. You need to include an assortment of these fabrics in your palette to contrast with

the medium- and dark-value fabrics you most likely already own. Remember that changes in value emphasize design elements; you need lighter-value fabrics to contrast with and accentuate medium- and darker-value fabrics.

Selecting Fabric Systematically

Selecting fabric can be organized into the process summarized on this flowchart.

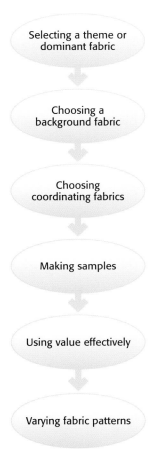

Selecting a theme or dominant fabric

Choosing a background fabric

Choosing coordinating fabrics

Making samples

Using value effectively

Varying fabric patterns

Tip Keep your project's theme in mind as you select fabrics. Refer to the notes you made during your brainstorming session. Design and fabric choices often evolve as we work through the overall process, but the theme remains constant.

Selecting a Theme or Dominant Fabric

For many projects, this is a "chicken-and-egg" type question: which came first, the wish to use a specific fabric, or a design idea that suggests a particular fabric? No matter which answer seems right to you, you will need to start by selecting a theme or dominant fabric for your quilt. This fabric will occupy a central place in the design units and/or in an outer border that pulls the overall quilt design together. This is the first fabric the viewer will notice when looking at the quilt.

Tip Some projects feature more than one theme fabric. For example, the theme of your quilt might be zebras on safari, and your dominant fabrics could be a fun print with running zebras, and a black-and-white zebra stripe.

As you consider fabrics for the theme or dominant fabric position, and later for the background and coordinating fabric positions, you will need to audition potential fabrics for the project. Take the theme fabrics out of your fabric palette and place them on your audition space. We have several requirements for a good auditioning space:

- Several square feet of uncluttered space. We like to use either an unused design board or a cleared dining room table.
- The space needs to be a neutral color, such as white or beige, so that the color of the design surface will not interfere with the fabric-selection process. We often cover the dining room table with a piece of white batting.
- Good, preferably natural, lighting, so that you can fully appreciate the value, texture, and color of individual fabrics.
- Space around the surface, so that you can step back at a distance for perspective.

Choosing a Background Fabric

The background fabric you choose sets the mood of your overall quilt design. The value of a background fabric is more important than the color itself, because its purpose is to move the viewer's eye around the quilt. The exception to this is when the background fabric is the principal design feature of the quilt. The background fabric is often the lightest- or the darkest-value fabric in the quilt, contrasting with and showing off the other fabrics.

The following photos show examples of horrible, bad, and good background fabric choices for the same quilt. The theme fabric in each example is a print that features black-and-white zebras on a pink background. In the first quilt, the background fabric is the black-and-white zebra stripe, which is so energetic that you hardly notice the pink Sawtooth Star shapes and small patches of color marching around the quilt, let alone the cute paw-print fabric in the centers of the stars.

Pink Zebra Fabric Quilt #1
Designed and pieced by Ann Castleberry, 1998, Gainesville, Florida, 30" x 30". Quilted by Cathy Leitner.

In this quilt, we decided to tone down the background by switching the zebra-stripe fabric with the paw-print fabric. The result is only a little more promising, but at least the Four Patch Star shapes and the marching patches of color are now noticeable. The black-and-white background print features the greatest degree of contrast; therefore, it is the one that catches the viewer's attention. As a background fabric, it is a slightly less aggravating choice than the zebra stripe, because there is significantly more white in the paw-print fabric. The problem with these first two quilts is that the viewer's eye is immediately drawn to the background and not engaged by the other elements in the quilt design.

Pink Zebra Fabric Quilt #2
Designed and pieced by Ann Castleberry, 1998, Gainesville, Florida, 30" x 30". Quilted by Cathy Leitner.

For this quilt, we threw out all the fabric choices from the first two quilts and started the systematic fabric-selection process over again. This time, we decided to emphasize the black-and-white nature of the zebras by using a black tone-on-tone fabric for the principal design feature—the central X, and the O shape that is created by the small squares and the inner border. We chose a tone-on-tone medium-blue fabric for the background fabric; it is the lightest-value fabric in the quilt. We incorporated small patches of a different black-and-white fabric in the background of the Four Patch Star shape. It is distracting but does not overwhelm the viewer.

Occasionally you may run across a fabric that is so wonderful and vibrant that you want to make it the focal point of a quilt, featuring it in large pieces so that it can be fully appreciated. These outstanding fabrics are typically multicolored prints with a large-scale, overall design such as an Asian, floral, or novelty print. A successful approach to using fabrics like these is to work with a very simple design, where the

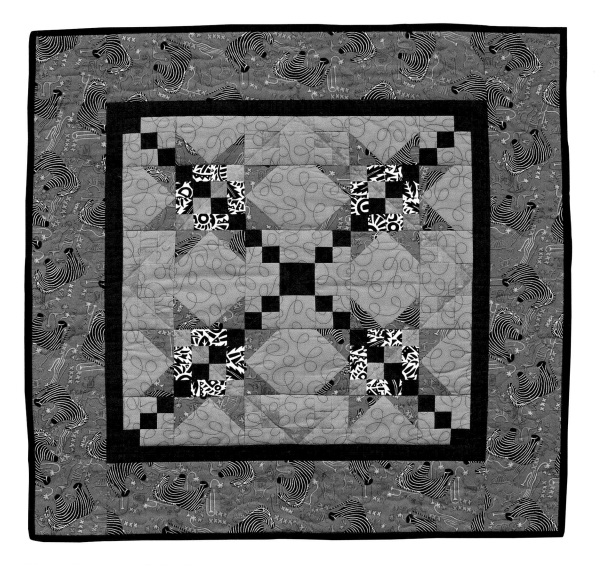

Pink Zebra Fabric Quilt #3
Designed and pieced by Ann Castleberry, 1998, Gainesville, Florida, 30" x 30". Quilted by Cathy Leitner.

background takes up half or more of the total surface area. An example would be the "Bugs!" quilt shown on page 88. Other guidelines for using a background fabric as the principal design feature in a quilt include the following:

- Make sure that the background fabric is either the lightest- or darkest-value fabric in the entire quilt so that the viewer's attention is immediately drawn to it.
- Use the background fabric in the outer border to complete the project and emphasize its importance in the overall design.
- Use a small number of low-energy, tone-on-tone, coordinating fabrics so that the background fabric does not get lost.

Choosing Coordinating Fabrics

Fabrics that coordinate with the theme fabric support it and call attention to the secondary design elements in a quilt. These lesser players do not reach out and grab the viewer's attention immediately; instead, they complement and enhance the theme fabric. Frequently, quilters choose coordinating fabrics by attempting to match the colors and values of the theme fabric exactly. The resultant fabric palette looks like a homogenous mix rather than an exciting array of values. Guidelines for selecting coordinating fabrics include the following:

- Identify the colors in the theme fabric (for example, rose and green).
- Choose a light, medium, and dark value of each color in the theme fabric, and audition them with the theme fabric.
- Stand back and view your fabric combinations. Analyze their suitability by comparing them with your drawing of the quilt design.
- Discard any fabrics that look out of place to you.

- Choose additional fabrics to fill in any gaps. Continue adding fabrics until you have more than you need for your project. You may need to try several combinations before you find the perfect choices.

Tip Tone-on-tone and small-scale floral or geometric prints always make good coordinating fabrics.

Making Samples

Sewing sample design units gives you the opportunity to check your fabric choices before you commit an appreciable amount of time and materials to making an entire quilt project. There are very few things more frustrating than cutting all of the pieces for a quilt and then deciding that you want or need to change or substitute some of them to achieve the look you want in the finished quilt. At best, constructing a few sample blocks and design units will confirm your good taste in choosing the best fabrics for your quilt. At worst, you will waste a few inches of fabric, which is much better than wasting a lot of fabric or making a project you will be less than happy with.

Tip Don't consider any of the sample blocks you make "wasted"; there is always something creative you can do with them in a future quilt project.

All of the quilts shown in this book feature just two to four simple shapes. We like to make several sample blocks or design units, place them on our design wall, and evaluate them. This approach of making basic components of a quilt in batches has three advantages:

- You don't get bored making the same block over and over.
- You can check your work to make sure that the proportions are correct. (Did you really mean to use 2½" rather than 2" connector squares?)
- You can check your value placements and fabric choices periodically.

Using Value Effectively

There are three guidelines for using value to create a dynamic quilt design:

- Use the darkest-value fabric to emphasize the primary design feature. Light and cool colors appear to recede visually, while dark, warm colors appear to advance.
- Making changes in value can accentuate primary designs and cause secondary designs to emerge.
- Value is more important than color in selecting fabrics.

These rules describe most, but not all, situations and provide structure for selecting fabrics appropriate for your quilt design.

> **Tip** Value emphasizes the design elements of a quilt, and color harmonizes the overall look or effect of the quilt.

Value can also be used to reinforce the symmetry of a quilt design. For example, the background grid in the "Tampas Go Hawaiian" quilt on page 84 features medium-value fabrics. Because the grid is not the primary design feature, we downplayed it with medium values.

The greatest possible contrast in value occurs when black and white occur in the same print, as shown in the three pink zebra quilts on pages 20–22. Because of this great difference in value, black-and-white fabrics tend to generate a lot of visual energy and naturally draw the viewer's eye. For that reason, black-and-white fabrics should be used sparingly in most quilts, because they can create too much chaos and detract from the quilt's design.

Varying Fabric Patterns

Including an array of different types of fabric patterns in a quilt increases its visual interest and helps to move the viewer's eye around the quilt. As shown in the photos of the three pink zebra quilts on pages 20–22, a higher degree of visual interest occurs when two different types of fabric patterns occur beside each other. For example, a swirly print next to a tone-on-tone fabric with geometric shapes is more visually interesting than two same-value solid fabrics placed side by side.

Another advantage to including a variety of fabric patterns and print scales in your quilt is that it tends to make small sewing imperfections less noticeable. For example, it is more difficult to spot a mismatched seam between two floral prints than between two solid fabrics.

It's fun to break all the rules we learned as children about combining fabrics in garments. For example, when it comes to making quilts, stripes really do work well with polka dots. A good way to learn more about creative ways to combine different fabric patterns in quilts is to check advertisements for complete fabric lines. Manufacturers typically include several pattern textures in each of their fabric lines.

^{c h a p t e r}

4

Working Through the Design Process

This chapter examines creative ways to work with a specific shape or pattern and choose fabrics to fit that pattern, as well as ways to move logically through a simple design progression to create complex, beautiful quilt designs.

In each of the quilts shown in chapters 4 and 5, only three shapes are used to create the overall quilt design. All of the quilts in this book are based on square and rectangular blocks that can be created by combining squares, rectangles, and half-square triangles in various ways. We have used a classic approach to quilt design, following these guidelines:

- The human eye enjoys repetition and symmetry. We used both of these elements to create interesting placements of design units and values in the overall quilt designs, as well as in choosing fabrics for each project.
- The focal point of a quilt design does not need to be in the exact center of the quilt. However, a central focal point does provide a starting point for establishing symmetry.
- A great quilt design can be accomplished with a few design units or combinations of blocks, as is illustrated by the projects in this book. You do not need a large number of design units to create a complex and visually satisfying design.
- Inner borders can enhance or complete a quilt design. For example, using the background fabric in the inner border creates the illusion that the quilt center is "floating" on the background fabric.

- The outer border can effectively accentuate the theme fabric. A pieced outer border can pull together all the fabrics used in the project.

Note: The fabric requirements and construction instructions for many of the quilts shown in chapters 4 and 5 are included following chapter 7.

Puss Design Progression

The design unit known as Puss in the Corner has been around since the beginning of the twentieth century. According to Barbara Brackman's classic *Encyclopedia of Pieced Quilt Patterns,* this traditional design unit (originally known as Aunt Sukey's Patch) was first published in 1914 in the *Household Journal.* The Puss in the Corner design unit is a nine patch, consisting of a plain center square surrounded by four chevron Puss blocks and Four Patch blocks in the corners.

Puss in the Corner design unit

The following Puss design progression includes five quilts. In creating them, we focused on the following two steps in the flow-chart process for creating secondary designs (page 13): sharing corners to create additional opportunities for secondary designs, and changing value to highlight specific shapes in a quilt design.

Puss in the Corner

"Puss in the Corner" features three simple shapes:

- Squares in the center of the Puss in the Corner design units and in the Four Patch blocks

- Triangles in the Puss blocks
- Rectangles in the Puss blocks and Four Patch blocks

Design unit

The quilt features twelve Puss in the Corner design units arranged side by side in four rows of three design units each. Each design unit consists of 9 blocks, as described above, for a total of 108 individual blocks needed to complete this quilt. These 108 blocks consist of 12 plain squares, 48 Four Patch blocks, and 48 Puss blocks.

We did not have a specific design theme or theme fabric that we wanted to showcase in this project; we wanted to create a traditional-looking quilt with a light background and contrasting accent colors. We chose jewel tones because we like working with them and have lots of choices in our fabric palettes. The Puss in the Corner design units appear to float on the background, because we also used the background fabric in the inner border. We didn't have a coordinating fabric to use in the middle border, so we pieced a border in the same fabrics we used in the Puss in the Corner design units. We finished the quilt with an outer border of the background fabric to emphasize the floating effect.

Puss in the Corner

Pieced by Carol Stanley, 1999, Gainesville, Florida, 50" x 62". Quilted by Adrienne Tavares. For project instructions, see page 68.

Plain Jane Pusses
(aka Puss Shares a Corner)

"Plain Jane Pusses" features three simple shapes:

- Squares in the center of the Puss in the Corner design units and in the corner blocks
- Triangles in the Puss blocks
- Rectangles in the Puss blocks

Design unit

The line drawings for "Plain Jane Pusses," "Secondary Sawtooth Stars," and "Flower Power Pusses" are all the same; the quilts look quite different, however, because we changed the placement of value and color in each one. Removing the Four Patch blocks from the Puss in the Corner design unit provided the opportunity for two Puss in the Corner design units to break into each other, or "share a corner." For this quilt, we wanted to emphasize the Puss "stars" floating in outer space. We started with a great background fabric of tiny, primary-colored stars on black and then used fat quarters from our stashes. Again, we used background fabric for the inner and outer borders to enhance the "floating" concept and a pieced border to tie together the Puss stars.

Plain Jane Pusses
Designed by Mischele Hart, pieced by Becky Valcante, 1999, Gainesville, Florida, 47" x 59". Quilted by Cathy Leitner. For project instructions, see page 70.

Secondary Sawtooth Stars

"Secondary Sawtooth Stars" features three simple shapes:

- Squares in the center of the Puss in the Corner design units and in the corner blocks
- Triangles in the Puss blocks
- Rectangles in the Puss blocks

The background fabric for both "Secondary Sawtooth Stars" and the next quilt, "Flower Power Pusses," is a pleasant, open, floral print

Design unit

featuring rose and violet-blue flowers with green leaves on a cream background. We chose rose and violet-blue fabrics to complement the floral print. For "Secondary Sawtooth Stars," we emphasized the Four Patch Star shape by using a medium violet-blue fabric for the Four Patch Star plain center block, with a darker violet-blue for the points in the Star Points plain blocks.

Secondary Sawtooth Stars
Designed, pieced, and quilted by Mischele Hart, 2000, Tampa, Florida, 26" x 26".

Flower Power Pusses

"Flower Power Pusses" features three simple shapes:

Design unit

- Squares in the center of the Puss in the Corner design units and in the corner blocks
- Triangles in the Puss blocks
- Rectangles in the Puss blocks

Sharing corners creates a diagonal look, which increases the interest of the overall design and creates an interesting opportunity for the secondary Four Patch Star shapes that emerge in "Flower Power Pusses." For this quilt, we chose our coordinating or supporting fabrics from two color families: rose and violet-blue. We used analogous color families (i.e. next to each other on the color wheel) to accentuate the star shapes, because the colors create tension that highlights the differences in placements of shapes and values.

Flower Power Pusses
Designed, pieced, and quilted by Mischele Hart, 2000, Tampa, Florida, 26" x 26".

Star-Studded Gecko Pusses

"Star-Studded Gecko Pusses" features three simple shapes:

- Triangles in the Puss blocks, Star Points plain blocks, and Square in a Square blocks
- Rectangles in the Puss blocks and Star Points plain blocks
- Squares in the Square in a Square blocks and the corner blocks

Design unit

We wanted to end the Puss progression by making one additional change—substituting a Square in a Square block for the plain center block in the Puss in the Corner design unit. The result is this "Star-Studded Gecko Pusses" quilt. We chose a fun conversation print featuring geckos as our theme fabric and selected supporting players from two different color families: yellow, orange, and red for the Puss in the Corner design units and yellow-green for the Four Patch Star triangle shapes. We wanted to show how to use a conversation print as a background fabric, so we placed the gecko fabric inside the Puss in the Corner design unit for the inner triangles, as well as the plain corner blocks. Substituting the Square in a Square blocks for the plain block centers enabled us to bring in more of the colors from the gecko fabric, and we were also trying to tone down the orange and yellow-green fabrics. Other interesting aspects of this quilt are the two visual "grids." The orange Puss blocks unite to produce a vivacious diagonal grid. It also appears that the yellow-green stars coalesce into a horizontal and vertical, or rectilinear, grid, which generates a calming influence on the overall visual effect of the project.

Star-Studded Gecko Pusses
Designed, pieced, and quilted by Mischele Hart, 1999, Tampa, Florida, 38" x 50". For project instructions, see page 72.

Tampas All in a Row Design Progression

The Tampa design unit is a simple variation of the Puss in the Corner design unit. In the Puss in the Corner design unit, the inner and outer triangles in the Puss block are the same size, and the resulting chevron lines run from the corner to the middle of the block. To create the Tampa block for this Tampa design unit, the inner triangle is reduced to half the size of the inner triangle in the Puss block. This small change in proportion creates a secondary design: a medallion center in the shape of an eight-pointed star in the middle of the Tampa design unit.

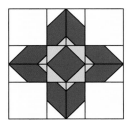

Tampa design unit

When Tampa design units are arranged in a traditional three-by-four layout, the area between them creates another, larger eight-pointed medallion shape. We have created six quilts in this design progression to explore this Tampas All in a Row arrangement. Two of the projects ("Pretty Tampas All in a Row" and "Tampa Windows") focus on using value changes within the traditional three-by-four design layout; four projects ("SnS Tampas," "Tampa Waterlilies," "Pretty Tampa Trellis I," and "Pretty Tampa Trellis II") focus on substituting different simple shapes for the plain block corners.

Pretty Tampas All in a Row
Designed by Ann Castleberry, pieced by Mischele Hart, 1999, Gainesville, Florida, 39" x 48". Quilted by Cathy Leitner. For project instructions, see page 74.

Pretty Tampas All in a Row

"Pretty Tampas All in a Row" features three simple shapes:

- Triangles in the Tampa blocks and Square in a Square blocks
- Rectangles in the Tampa blocks
- Squares in the Corner blocks

Design unit

This is the most basic of our Tampa quilts—a three-by-four arrangement of side-by-side Tampa design units and a single background fabric. The purpose of this quilt was to highlight the background fabric. As mentioned, the shared space between the design units forms an eight-pointed star shape that echoes the star shape in the center of the Tampa design units.

Because the background fabric is so lively, we sandwiched a simple pieced strip of red and blue between two rounds of background to complete the project. Anything more elaborate would have lessened the impact of the background fabric.

Tampa Windows

"Tampa Windows" features three simple shapes:

Design unit

- Triangles in the Tampa blocks and the Square in a Square blocks
- Rectangles in the Tampa blocks
- Squares in the Square in a Square blocks and the corner blocks

The line drawing for this quilt is the same as for the previous quilt; only the placement of values within the quilt design has changed. We wanted to emphasize the horizontal and vertical arrangement of the Tampa design units rather than the eight-pointed star or medallion shape between the units, so we used a lighter background fabric to suggest a feeling of the outdoors, with red and black to suggest mullions in a window. We added the turquoise print to the Square in a Square blocks to incorporate another color in the project and echoed the same print in the outer border.

Tampa Windows
Designed and pieced by Mischele Hart, 1999, Tampa, Florida, 35" x 43".
Quilted by Cathy Leitner.

SnS Tampas

"SnS Tampas" features three simple shapes:

- Rectangles in the Tampa blocks
- Squares in the Square in a Square blocks
- Triangles in the Tampa blocks, Square in a Square blocks; half-square triangles in the corner blocks

Our objective for this project was to substitute a Half-Square Triangle block for the plain corner blocks and then play with the resulting

Design unit

design possibilities. This allowed us to emphasize the similarity between the small red and large teal eight-pointed star or medallion shapes. Substituting the half-square triangles enabled us to create two Square in a Square shapes—the blocks in the center of the Tampa design units and the larger, four-block Square in a Square shape shared between two Tampa design units.

We varied the values to emphasize the contrasts between adjacent shapes. We used value to explore the dynamic secondary design possibilities for this project. In the Square in a Square blocks inside the Tampa design units, there are light centers with a darker-value medallion "ring" surrounding them. In the Square in a Square blocks created by the adjacent Tampa design units, there are dark centers surrounded by lighter "rings." In the inner border, a dark green fabric creates the "floating on the background" concept, and in the outer border, the theme fabric pulls together all of the colors used in the quilt.

SnS Tampas
Designed by Ann Castleberry, pieced by Sandra Sontag, 1999, Gainesville, Florida, 48" x 60".
Quilted by Cathy Leitner. For project instructions, see page 76.

Tampa Waterlilies

"Tampa Waterlilies" features three simple shapes:

- Rectangles in the Tampa blocks
- Triangles in the Tampa blocks and the Square in a Square blocks
- Squares in the Four Patch blocks and the Square in a Square blocks

We transformed the Tampa design units in this quilt by using Four Patch blocks to create a second, large, eight-pointed star shape that resembles the center of a flower. The Tampa

Design unit

block appears to create concentric eight-pointed star shapes. So we combined this flower shape with a water-lily conversation print to create this Tampa Waterlilies design. Again, this project is all about value placement. We used a light blue-violet background fabric for the "water," and chose a darker green for the "leaves and stems" in the Four Patch blocks and the centers of the Square in a Square blocks. The flowers appear to float on the watery background, and the light fabric in the inner border continues this design theme.

Tampa Waterlilies
Designed and pieced by Ann Castleberry, 1999, Gainesville, Florida, 35" x 44".
Quilted by Carol Leitner. For project instructions, see page 78.

Tip Increasing the size of the Pretty Tampa Trellis designs does not lessen their effectiveness. These quilts are a great choice when you want to make a large project that is fast and easy without losing the appeal of the original design. It's always easier to make twelve large design units than thirty-five small ones.

Pretty Tampa Trellis I

"Pretty Tampa Trellis I" features three simple shapes:

- Rectangles in the Tampa blocks
- Triangles in the Dugout blocks, the Tampa blocks, and the Square in a Square blocks
- Squares in the Square in a Square blocks and the Dugout blocks

Design unit

In this Pretty Tampa Trellis design, we substituted Dugout blocks for the plain corner squares in the Tampa design units. This quickly created a strong, energetic diagonal grid that evokes the look of a garden trellis.

Pretty Tampa Trellis I
Designed by Ann Castleberry, pieced by Sandy Pozzetta, 1999, Gainesville, Florida, 35" x 44".
Quilted by Cathy Leitner.

Pretty Tampa Trellis II

"Pretty Tampa Trellis II" features three simple shapes:

- Rectangles in the Tampa blocks
- Triangles in the Dugout blocks, the Square in a Square blocks, and the Tampa blocks
- Squares in the Square in a Square blocks and the Dugout blocks

Design unit

We are both fortunate enough to live in Florida, where it is possible to have flowers blooming in the garden all year round. Rather than using a fabric that looked like "wood" for the trellis grid in this quilt, we used a floral print to evoke the look of a constantly blooming trellis. We chose coordinating fabrics from the colors in the floral print for the Tampa and Square in a Square blocks and selected a dark background fabric to represent distant background space.

Pretty Tampa Trellis II
Designed by Ann Castleberry, pieced by Mischele Hart, 1999, Gainesville, Florida, 42" x 60". Quilted by Cathy Leitner. For project instructions, see page 80.

Tampas Connect Up Design Progression

In the Tampas Connect Up design progression we examine using common shapes in shared corners, creating additional design possibilities by substituting different blocks for plain corner squares, creating a background grid, and using value to change the emphasis within a quilt design. We simplified the Tampa design units so that adjacent units shared a corner, as shown in the illustration on page 13 in chapter 2. As in the Puss quilts, sharing a corner creates a secondary design of a Four Patch Star, and playing with the star shape and the plain squares between the Tampa blocks opens up a myriad of design possibilities.

Original Tampa Connects Up

"Original Tampa Connects Up" features three simple shapes:

- Rectangles in the Tampa blocks
- Triangles in the Tampa blocks and the Square in a Square blocks
- Squares in the Square in a Square blocks and the corner blocks

Design unit

This quilt was the original inspiration for this book, and we designed it to showcase our newly created Tampa design unit, which we named after Mischele's hometown. This design is simplified in terms of value and color in order to focus the viewer's eye on the Tampa shapes. We used similar values for the Tampa and Four Patch Star shapes; this creates a grid that makes the shapes appear to float on the background fabric. The wide outer border of background fabric emphasizes this floating effect. The grid appears to create multiple secondary design possibilities, such as the Maltese cross shapes created in the center of the quilt, as well as the Four Patch Star shapes.

Original Tampa Connects Up
Designed, pieced, and quilted by Mischele Hart, 1998, Tampa, Florida, 39" x 51". For project instructions, see page 82.

Tampas Go Hawaiian

"Tampas Go Hawaiian" features three simple shapes:

- Rectangles in the Tampa blocks
- Triangles in the Tampa blocks, the Dugout blocks, and the Square in a Square blocks
- Squares in the Square in a Square blocks and the Dugout blocks

Design unit

A single simple change from the "Original Tampa Connects Up" quilt creates a new set of design possibilities in this project: substituting Dugout blocks for the plain corner blocks in the shared corners creates a strongly diagonal grid. Orange and blue are complementary colors on the color wheel; these colors emphasize the differences between the Dugout blocks and the Tampa design units. The Four Patch Star and Dugout shapes feature three values of turquoise that produce the diagonal grid.

Each of the Tampa "stars" is a combination of yellow-orange (called cheddar), fuchsia pink, and purple. The dark purple background fabric "peeks out" from each Tampa, accentuating the idea that the design is floating across the background. Using an inner border of background fabric completes the "floating across the background" idea. The wild and exuberant Hawaiian fabric used in the outer border is tamed by a small pieced border of pink and purple between the outer and inner borders.

An X and O approach was used to select the fabric for this quilt. The diagonal grid creates many Xs for this project. So we used a "trip around the world" or "barn-raising" approach for the Tampa units. We used light pink, purple, and cheddar fabrics for the center Tampa unit. Then we used medium pink, purple, and cheddar fabrics for the center ring of Tampa units. Finally, we used dark pink, purple, and cheddar fabrics for the outer ring of units.

Tampas Go Hawaiian
Designed, pieced, and quilted by Ann Castleberry, 1998, Gainesville, Florida, 45" x 45".
For project instructions, see page 84.

This step within the design progression includes the following:

- Four blocks: Square in a Square, Tampa, Dugout, and Star Points plain
- Four fabric color groups: dark background, coordinating floral for the outer border, cheddar for the Tampas, and turquoise for the diagonal grid created by the Dugout and Four Patch Star shapes
- X and O approach to selecting final fabrics

Tampa Christmas Poinsettias

"Tampa Christmas Poinsettias" features three simple shapes:

- Rectangles in the Tampa blocks
- Triangles in the Tampa blocks, the Square in a Square blocks, and the Star Points plain blocks
- Squares in the Square in a Square blocks and the Four Patch blocks

Design unit

As in the "Tampa Waterlilies" quilt shown on page 78, substituting Four Patch blocks for the plain corner blocks creates a flower shape. The red and green fabrics in the flower shapes, combined with an outer border of poinsettia fabric, create a wonderful Christmas quilt. The poinsettias appear to float on a black background that looks like a night sky, an effect that is further enhanced by the black fabric in the narrow inner border.

Tampa Christmas Poinsettias
Designed and pieced by Ann Castleberry, 1998, Gainesville, Florida, 45" x 45".
Quilted by Cathy Leitner. For project instructions, see page 86.

Tampa Magic Carpet

"Tampa Magic Carpet" features three simple shapes:

- Rectangles in the Tampa blocks
- Triangles in the Tampa blocks, the Square in a Square blocks, and the Star Points plain blocks
- Squares in the Square in a Square blocks and the corner blocks

Design unit

Our purpose in making this project was to de-emphasize the Tampa units and emphasize the points in the Star Points plain blocks and the background fabric. Unlike in the previous quilts, we used fabrics with all the same values, and a wild Hawaiian-print background fabric to mimic the look of carpeting. Can you think of other ways to de-emphasize the Tampa blocks and emphasize the background?

Tampa Magic Carpet
Designed and pieced by Ann Castleberry, 1999, Gainesville, Florida, 42" x 54".
Quilted by Cathy Leitner.

Exploring the Four Patch Star Design Progression

The focus of this chapter is the design progression based on the Four Patch Star design unit, which features the traditional Sawtooth Star shape. We created each of the following quilt designs using one to three of the steps from the design flowchart on page 13. We included nine quilts in this design progression. Each one looks quite different from the others, though they are all related.

The number of design possibilities you can create with the Four Patch Star design unit is literally endless. You can vary a project theme, change proportions of shapes (for example, combining little stars with large plain blocks versus making all blocks the same size), alter value placements, and use fabric and color in innovative ways to create quilts that are entirely your own creations.

Basic Four Patch Star Design Progression

The purpose of the first two projects in this design progression is to build on the basic concept presented in Mary Ellen Hopkins' Four Patch Star design. We tied the stars together by adding a horizontal and vertical grid. We also played with value. Remember, our eyes are drawn to the darkest value, so the Four Patch Stars stand out when they are made with the darkest-value fabric. What stands out the most is that each of the quilts looks different. You wouldn't know they were based on the same design unit if we didn't tell you.

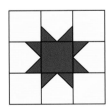

Four Patch Star design unit

Darling, Those Bugs Have Legs!

"Darling, Those Bugs Have Legs!" features three simple shapes:

- Rectangles in the Star Points plain blocks and alternating blocks
- Triangles in the Star Points plain blocks
- Squares in the corner blocks

Design unit

This quilt was made using the Four Patch Star pattern presented in Mary Ellen Hopkins's book #4, *Connecting Up*. The quilt name refers to the great potential for design variations using this single gem of an idea—there are more possibilities than there are legs on a bug! To select the fabrics for this quilt, we started our brainstorming process with the great bug fabric. The stars are the principal design feature, so we chose fabrics with a darker value than the bug print for points in the Star Points plain blocks.

Darling, Those Bugs Have Legs!

Designed by Mary Ellen Hopkins. Pieced and quilted by Mischele Hart. Tampa, Florida, 2000, 32" x 38".

Yellow Floral Sweetie

"Yellow Floral Sweetie" features three simple shapes:

- Rectangles in the Star Points plain blocks
- Triangles in the Star Points plain blocks
- Squares in the plain blocks and Four Patch Star centers

Design unit

Just adding a strongly horizontal and vertical background grid and changing the theme fabric creates an entirely different look in this "Yellow Floral Sweetie" quilt. The Four Patch Stars do not appear to float on the background; instead, the grid extends all the way to the inner border, which ties the project together. Again, the principal design feature is the stars, so we used fabrics with the darkest values in the Four Patch Star centers and Star Points plain blocks.

Yellow Floral Sweetie
Designed, pieced, and quilted by Mischele Hart, 1999, Tampa, Florida, 32" x 38".

Adding Horizontal and Vertical Grids with Rail Blocks

We made two changes to the "Yellow Floral Sweetie" design to create "Bugs!": we substituted a Rail block for the rectangular block used in the horizontal and vertical grid, and we changed the relative proportions of the blocks.

Bugs!

"Bugs!" features three simple shapes:

- Rectangles in the Star Points Rail blocks
- Triangles in the Star Points Rail blocks
- Squares in the plain blocks and Four Patch Star centers

For the "Bugs!" quilt, we wanted to use both the asymmetrical black-and-white striped fabric

Design unit

and the yellow-green fabric with the bug print; however, solid sashing strips of either one might have been overwhelming. Surprisingly, the effectiveness of both fabrics is enhanced when the two are combined in the Rail-block sashing strips. The yellow-green fabric in the Rail blocks is the color complement of the orange-red Four Patch Stars; the pairing creates visual harmony.

The Four Patch Star centers are 2" finished, and the large plain blocks of bug fabric are 6" finished; these dimensions set up a rectangle for the Rail block of 2" x 6". The ½" finished yellow-green strip is sandwiched between two ¾" finished strips of the black-and-white striped fabric, which helps to tone down the yellow-green fabric. We chose these relative proportions to show off the bug fabric to best advantage.

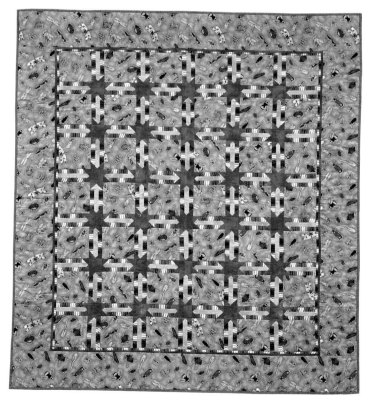

Bugs!
Designed, pieced, and quilted by Mischele Hart, 1999, Tampa, Florida, 59" x 67".
For project instructions, see page 88.

Salute to the Fourth of July

"Salute to the Fourth of July" features three simple shapes:

- Rectangles in the Star Points Rail blocks
- Triangles in the Star Points Rail blocks
- Squares in the plain blocks and Four Patch Star centers

Design unit

As in the first two quilts in this progression, the principal design feature in this quilt is the Four Patch Star. Therefore, we used the darkest-value fabric for the points in the Star Points Rail blocks. We chose dark navy and white for the Rail blocks to create the narrow horizontal and vertical grid of sashing strips, suggesting stripes. Look carefully, and you will notice that we placed white and blue star-center fabrics in concentric rings or Os starting in the center of the quilt. The red Four Patch Star points are also arranged in concentric Os. We modified the relative proportions between the Four Patch Star centers and plain blocks to 3" and 4" respectively, to create a slightly asymmetrical perspective to this quilt since there was not a single fabric we wanted to highlight. The quilt finishes with a simple border of the navy background fabric. No additional border appeared necessary.

Salute to the Fourth of July
Designed and pieced by Ann Castleberry, 1998, Gainesville, Florida, 37" x 65".
Quilted by Cathy Leitner.

Adding Energy: Incorporating Diagonal Lines

Two simple changes add extra energy to the overall design of the following two quilts: substituting a Dugout block for the plain or "empty" block enabled us to incorporate a diagonal grid into the overall design, and substituting the Square in a Square block for every other Four Patch Star center introduced an interesting new visual element. Surprisingly, the line drawings for these two quilts are identical— the only difference is the relative proportion between the Four Patch Star centers and the Dugout blocks. In "Circus Tents," all the blocks are same-size squares, while in "Floral Tents," the Four Patch Star centers are 3" and Dugout blocks are 5" finished.

We highlighted the horizontal and vertical grid in both quilts by placing the background fabric and accent fabric in the Rail blocks. Because of the way we used value and color in both quilts, it appears that each design features horizontal and vertical and diagonal grids with stars floating above them.

Circus Tents

"Circus Tents" features three simple shapes:

- Rectangles in the Star Points Rail blocks
- Triangles in the Star Points Rail blocks, the Dugout blocks, and the Square in a Square blocks
- Squares in the Four Patch Star centers, the Square in a Square blocks, and the Dugout blocks

Design unit

With its bold, primary-colored fabrics, "Circus Tents" is a fun quilt. We subtitled it "Stripes and Polka Dots Do Go Together." We used the striped fabric for the inside rectangles in the Rail blocks and red and blue polka-dot fabrics for the Four Patch Star centers and Dugout blocks. Alternating plain blocks with Square in a Square blocks creates two different looking Four Patch Stars using the same simple shape.

Circus Tents
Designed and pieced by Ann Castleberry, 1999, Gainesville, Florida, 33" x 45". Quilted by Mischele Hart. For project instructions, see page 90.

Floral Tents

"Floral Tents" features three simple shapes:

- Rectangles in the Star Points Rail blocks
- Triangles in the Star Points Rail blocks, the Square in a Square blocks, and the Dugout blocks
- Squares in the Four Patch Star centers, the Square in a Square blocks, and the Dugout blocks

Design unit

The effect of alternating Square in a Square blocks in every other Four Patch Star center is enhanced in "Floral Tents" by the green fabric in the Square in a Square block center and the horizontal and vertical grid and the pink fabric in the plain Four Patch Star centers and the diagonal grid.

Tip One useful-to-know trick we used in this project is something we call "When you don't want to match seams, miss by a mile and it will look like you meant it!" It can be challenging to match seams when several points come together, as they do in this design. One tricky matching point could have been where the Dugout blocks meet the Star Points Rail blocks. We deliberately designed the quilt so the connector shapes would not match up.

Floral Tents

Designed by Ann Castleberry and Mischele Hart, pieced by Donna Sappington, and quilted by ruthie miller, 1998, Tampa, Florida, 40" x 54". For project instructions, see page 92.

Introducing Variations on Blocks: Snowball Blocks and Hole in the Wall Blocks

For added interest, use block variations, such as Snowball and Hole in the Wall blocks, in design units. The Snowball block is a variation of the

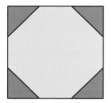
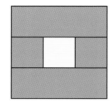

Snowball block   Hole in the Wall block

Square in a Square block. The proportion of the triangle shape to the center block is smaller. As shown in the illustration left, Hole in the Wall block is one of the more unusual nine-patch variations.

Introducing Hole in the Wall blocks and deleting the Star Points led to the next two designs, known affectionately as "Jungle Sprockets" and "Turquoise Tango." The horizontal and vertical grid in each quilt consists of the traditional arrangement of background and accent fabric in the Rail blocks, alternating with Hole in the Wall blocks. The diagonal grids in both quilts consist of Snowball blocks connected by Dugout blocks. The horizontal and vertical grids in both quilts feature Rail blocks and Hole in the Wall blocks.

Jungle Sprockets

"Jungle Sprockets" features three simple shapes:

- Rectangles in the Rail blocks and the Hole in the Wall blocks
- Triangles in the Snowball blocks and the Dugout blocks
- Squares in the Dugout blocks, Hole in the Wall blocks, and the Snowball blocks

Design unit

In "Jungle Sprockets," the lime green fabric in the Snowball block at the center of the quilt is also featured in the adjacent Dugout blocks. The juxtaposition creates an X configuration that continues beyond the orange fabric in the Snowball blocks and Dugout blocks that create the O configuration. A horizontal and vertical grid is created using dark brown fabric in the center of the Rail

Jungle Sprockets
Designed and pieced by Ann Castleberry, 1998, Gainesville, Florida, 32" x 43". Quilted by Shirley Swanson.

and the Hole in the Wall block. Both the diagonal and the horizontal and vertical grid appear to be floating on the background, and the background fabric in the inner border enhances this effect. A pieced outer border ties the colors together and neatly completes the quilt.

Turquoise Tango

"Turquoise Tango" features three simple shapes:

- Rectangles in the Rail blocks and the Hole in the Wall blocks
- Triangles in the Snowball blocks

- Squares in the Hole in the Wall blocks, the Snowball blocks, and the Dugout blocks

Design unit

In "Turquoise Tango," the yellow fabric in the diagonal grid creates an X configuration that reaches from the center of the quilt to the corners. An orange fabric highlights the diagonal O configuration, and the green fabric links both the yellow and orange configurations together, balancing the effect of the diagonal grid. The Hole in the Wall blocks and Rail blocks in the horizontal and vertical grid are highlighted by a blue fabric.

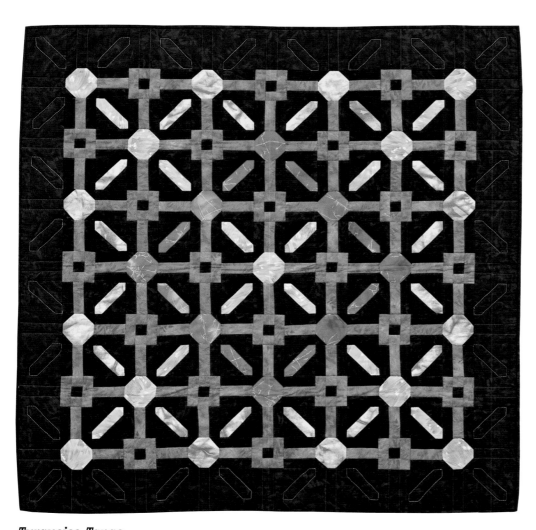

Turquoise Tango
Designed and pieced by Mischele Hart, 1999, Tampa, Florida, 47" x 47".
Quilted by Jackie Robinson. For project instructions, see page 94.

Expanding the Grid: Adding More Blocks

Rethinking the overall Four Patch Star design suggested an interesting alternative. What if we added blocks so that there were four blocks between every juncture in the grid? An example of expanding the grid is shown in "Christmas Surprise Boxes."

Christmas Surprise Boxes

"Christmas Surprise Boxes" features three simple shapes:

- Rectangles in the Rail blocks

- Triangles in the Snowball blocks and the Dugout blocks
- Squares in the Snowball blocks and the Dugout blocks

Design unit

We established a horizontal and vertical grid using the Rail block combination of a strong, red center rail sandwiched between two rails of light background fabric. The gold and dark green Snowball shapes are meant to suggest the look of holiday packages wrapped with red ribbon. We inserted four Dugout blocks between the Snowball "bows," and the X configurations of the Dugout blocks suggested folded wrapping paper on the sides of the packages. The diagonal grid in this quilt works in two ways visually. First, it creates Xs within a box formed by the Snowball blocks. Second, it creates smaller boxes if you view the quilt from a 45° angle. An inner border of the red fabric used in the horizontal and vertical grid surrounds the diagonal grids. The entire quilt is completed with a festive holiday-print outer border.

Christmas Surprise Boxes
Designed and pieced by Ann Castleberry, 1999, Gainesville, Florida, 36" x 45". Quilted by Mischele Hart.

Exploring These Concepts in Your Projects

We have just scratched the surface for the design progression in this chapter; the possibilities remain endless. You would need a mountain of fabric and a bevy of very busy elves to create all the quilts you could think up with these ideas as starting points. However, all of the quilt designs in this chapter boil down to the following ideas:

• Use squares for plain blocks, rectangles in Rail blocks, and triangle shapes for Square in a Square blocks, Snowball blocks, Star Points blocks, and Dugout blocks.

• Add a horizontal and vertical grid to create structure for a quilt design; something on which you can "hang" the remaining design and fabric elements.

• Add a diagonal grid to create visual energy and exuberance in a quilt design.

• Use the darkest-value fabric to emphasize the principal design element.

• Change the relative proportions between Four Patch Star centers and squares to showcase a specific fabric.

6

Try It—You Might Like It!

After working through the design progressions in chapters 4 and 5, you have a solid foundation for exploring your potential in creating original quilt designs. In this chapter, we want to give you some advice and encouragement based on our experiences teaching design workshops throughout the country and working in our own studios.

Design Challenge—Not Design Problem!

There's something to be said for putting a cheery face on life's little speed bumps. Your mother was right; it does take fewer muscles to smile than to frown! The ideas we present in this book are all about quilting, which is something we do in our leisure time to express the creative person within each of us. As it is for the majority of quilters, quiltmaking is also an activity that refreshes our souls. In the end, what we really want is to create something that makes us smile a little more. Relax and have some fun with the design processes presented in this book. Think of creating a new quilt design as an opportunity to grow and stretch your creative muscles.

If you find yourself absolutely stuck and a project has ceased to be fun, simply put it down for awhile and ask for opinions or sympathy from a quilting friend. Or abandon the project entirely! "What? Abandon a project?" you ask. What about all the time and money you invested in it? Sometimes the smartest thing you can do is to just cut your losses and move on to another project. Why spend time beating your head against a wall? Life is too short to spend precious leisure hours becoming frustrated. We hate to see one of our students realize that a project is not going to work out the way she wanted, yet be unable to stop because "wasting" fabric doesn't seem right.

What about Wasting Fabric?

Take a moment to think about why wasting fabric seems more important than wasting your precious leisure time. Which one do you have more of? We both have a lot more fabric in our stashes than we will ever be able to use in our lifetimes. (Don't tell that to our husbands—we would simply deny it!) And what's more, we will probably never stop adding to our fabric collections. (We like to call this process "expanding our personal fabric palettes.") And here is a concept for consideration: when you die, your spouse (or children or whoever) is most likely going to sell your entire stash at a yard sale for $1 per yard! That's right, your favorite batik that you saved for eleven years might well land up in a Halloween clown outfit for someone else's child.

Don't ever feel guilty about abandoning a project that seems frustrating to you in some way, or one that you simply do not want to spend any more time on. Donate projects like these to your local quilt guild for an annual white elephant sale, finish the project as a small lap quilt and donate it to a local hospital—or make a new padded throne for your cat.

> T<small>IP</small>   Remember—your time is always more precious than fabric!

Decreasing Your Design Anxieties

This book provides you with a nonthreatening, structured approach to designing a quilt and selecting fabric. The flowcharts give you a starting and ending point for each stage along the way. You don't need to use the results that come from doing every step in each process, nor do you need to feel obligated to make quilts from all of the ideas you develop. What you can do is pick and choose the parts of the design process that work best for you and take advantage of those in designing your quilts. Without exception, we think it is worthwhile to begin each project with a personal brainstorming session, so that you can "explain" to yourself all the reasons you have for making the quilt. This will make you feel comfortable spending your valuable time on it. Remember that you are not looking for deep rationalizations to emerge from this type of brainstorming. Typically, the reasons for making a particular project are simple, such as, "I need a sample for a class I'm going to teach," or "I want to know what happens if I substitute a Four Patch block for the Dugout block in a particular quilt design." All you need to get started is that kernel of an idea or an initial plan. Your creativity will take over from there.

Always, Always, Always Make Samples!

We never start a project without making a small sample of the blocks and design units we want to incorporate in it. Since very few people can look at a pile of fabric and imagine a finished quilt top, we think it is extremely important to take time to evaluate some samples of the various blocks and design units you want to feature in your project. It usually takes only a few strips of fabric and an hour or two of your time to do this. If you like the samples you've created, you are ready to move on to cutting and sewing the quilt top. And if you don't like them, now is the time to modify them as you wish, before you invest time, effort, or materials in making the quilt.

We use small samples that don't work out in one of our quilt projects as teaching samples for our workshops; sometimes, the "wrong" thing can be a more valuable teaching tool than the "right" one. For example, you might use small samples of blocks to illustrate a need for greater contrast in values between Dugout blocks and your background fabric.

We all learn in different ways. Some people simply listen to the teacher and can immediately form a picture in their minds. Others are visual learners and can easily work out an approach after looking at the directions. We are both "learning-by-doing" people—we need to actually feel the fabric and work through making an example before we feel comfortable making a project. Our biggest mistakes have usually occurred when we mistakenly thought that an idea was foolproof and didn't bother with making samples.

No Discomfort, No Growth!

That old saying, "No pain, no gain!" applies to quilting, too. When we choose to take the route of no discomfort, such as making a quilt from a pattern or book, we may also be choosing to hamper creative growth in ourselves. Developing new design skills can sometimes be uncomfortable; you will have to stretch and learn new skills. And you will need to face in advance that not every project you create may inspire a "wow" reaction in you; some of your designs may seem just ho-hum. Look through the quilts shown in this book; some of them might make you say, "wow," while others might inspire you to think, "Why did she make that one?" Interestingly, no two quilters would probably agree on which of our quilts in this book fall into those two categories. One person's "ho-hum" quilt is often another person's "wow."

Tip Remember that not every quilt you design will be a star—but every design you create will be worth your investment of time and effort if you learn something.

The more experience you gain in designing quilts, the more your perceptions will evolve and the greater your skills will become. Have you seen the T-shirt that says "Age and Treachery Always Beat Youth and Speed"? We need to look at quilting from that same perspective. What you are capable of today is not what you will be able to do next year. Make it a habit to spend time alone in your studio (always think of it as a "studio" and not as a "sewing room"!) and work out your quilt designs to suit yourself. Many of us, especially women, tend to spend too much time listening to "doubting Thomases" in our lives and not enough time listening to the "You can do it!" voice inside each of us. You do have the ability to create wonderful and unique quilt projects. We have watched many students do just that—and if they can, so can you! Good luck, and have fun as you play and experiment with our systematic approach to designing quilts and selecting fabrics. Use the quick-and-easy construction techniques in chapter 7 to make the quilt projects that follow, and enjoy designing your own quilts with our methods and techniques. We are always interested in seeing our students' work, so please send us pictures of your finished quilts. Who knows? We may even include your work in our next book!

Construction Techniques

This chapter contains general sewing tips and directions for making the blocks featured in the projects in this book, for assembling a quilt top with our four-patch method, for layering and basting a quilt sandwich, and for finishing techniques.

Accurate Machine Piecing

We all want our finished quilt tops to lie perfectly flat, with seams and points that match perfectly and without lumps, bubbles, or wiggles. The more precision you use in cutting, sewing, and pressing the individual blocks of your quilt, the more likely your quilt top is to be both straight and true. The single most important aspect of quilt construction is an accurate and consistent ¼" seam allowance, because the difference between a scant ¼" and a generous ¼" seam allowance can add up to a significant discrepancy across a pieced quilt top.

Sewing an accurate ¼" seam allowance depends on the sewing machine and the presser foot you use, the position of the needle, the shape of the hole in the needle plate (round, single hole, or wider hole for zigzag stitching), and your own height. The first step toward accurate machine piecing is to check your own sewing situation. Then try the following ¼" seam-allowance test.

1. Cut five 2" x 6" strips of fabric from 2 or more contrasting fabrics.
2. Arrange the strips next to your sewing machine so that adjacent colors are contrasting.
3. Sew the 5 strips together.
4. On an ironing board, use a hot iron on the cotton setting to press the seams toward the darker fabrics.
5. Measure the finished width of the sewn strips. Also measure the width across the 5 joined strips; if you sewed your ¼" seam allowance accurately, this measurement should be 8". Each of the inner strips should measure 1½", and the 2 outer strips should be 1¾" wide.

It is not unusual to need to repeat this exercise three or four times before your strip widths are accurate and consistent. We still repeat this exercise periodically, just to check our machine piecing accuracy and consistency.

Tip Make it a habit to clean your sewing machine and change the needle each time you sit down to make a new quilt project.

Pressing Matters

Take a few minutes before you begin sewing any project to determine the pressing directions you want for the blocks and design units in your quilt. As a general rule, press toward the darker fabric whenever possible, and press adjacent seam allowances in opposite directions, so that the seams will nest together easily as you sew them together, creating minimal bulk in your quilt top. For example, consider whether you might want to press the outer two strips in a Rail block toward the center rectangle because the adjacent block contains a connector square. We both find it helpful to do line drawings of our design units and add directional arrows that show the pressing directions we've chosen.

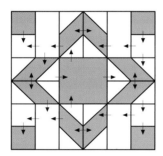

Pressing directions

Tip When you make sample blocks for your quilt, it will often be immediately clear which way you should press the seam allowances; when you are assembling your quilt top, you can still re-press certain seam allowances if necessary.

Constructing Blocks

After you have learned how to construct the following blocks, refer to the individual project instructions for cutting directions and the total number of blocks required for each project.

Plain Blocks

Not much needs to be said about plain blocks. They are simply squares cut to the correct sizes for a project. The best thing about them is that you can press them in any direction. We often press seam allowances toward plain blocks because they contain no additional seam allowances that could cause bulk.

Plain block

Four Patch Blocks

As the name implies, Four Patch blocks consist of four squares sewn together. Fortunately, it is hardly ever necessary to sew four individual squares together to create a Four Patch block; Four Patch blocks are usually made using strip sets, as described here:

Note: For "Puss in the Corner" (page 68), you do need to sew together individual squares.

1. Refer to the project directions to determine the number and finished size of the Four Patch blocks required for the project you want to make.
2. Refer to the project cutting chart. Cut the required number of strips the specified width by 42" in each of the colors called for in your project.
3. Sew strip sets together as directed in the project, placing appropriate colors together.

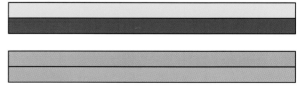

Two strip sets for a Four Patch block

4. Press the seam allowances so that they will oppose each other or "lock together" in the finished Four Patch block.
5. Cut each strip set into segments as directed in the cutting chart.

6. Sew segments together in pairs as needed for your project.

Four Patch

7. If the project you want to make features Four Patch blocks that contain rectangles, refer to the cutting directions and cut the number of strips you need; cut these strips into rectangles and sew each rectangle to a step 5 segment to create Four Patch blocks like these.

Four Patch
with rectangle

Rail Blocks

Rail blocks are even easier to make than Four Patch blocks, because they do not have a center seam that needs to be matched. Simply sew together the strips needed for your Rail block and cut them to the size required for your project. Rail blocks can be square or rectangular, depending on the way they are used in a project. Follow these steps to make Rail blocks.

Tip Remember that the three strips in a Rail block do not need to be the same width. To emphasize a particular value or color, you can make one or more of the strips wider than the others.

1. Refer to the project directions to determine the number of Rail blocks needed for your project and the widths of the individual strips within the block.
2. Refer to the project cutting chart. Cut the required number of strips in the specified widths and colors.
3. Sew the first 2 strips of the Rail strip sets together.

4. Press the seam allowance according to your pressing plan for your project.
5. Sewing in the opposite direction to minimize distortions, sew the third strip to the 2 joined strips.

6. Press the seam allowance as needed for your project.
7. Cut the strip set into segments in the widths needed for the Rail blocks in your project.

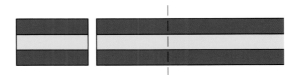

Using "Connector" Squares to Create Triangle Shapes

Blocks that contain triangle shapes, such as Puss blocks, Tampa blocks, Dugout blocks, Snowball blocks, Square in a Square blocks, and Star Points blocks, are constructed using either two or four smaller "connector" squares that are stitched diagonally from corner to corner to join them to a larger square or rectangle. Puss blocks are made with two background rectangles that each have two same-size connector squares sewn to them in opposite directions; the rectangles are sewn together to form the Puss block. Tampa blocks are made in the same manner, but with two background rectangles that have two different sizes of connector squares sewn to them in opposite directions; the rectangles are sewn together to form the Tampa block. Star Points plain blocks and Dugout blocks consist of one background square and two connector squares, while Snowball and Square in a Square blocks require one background square and four connector squares. Follow these steps to sew triangle shapes easily and quickly for any of these blocks.

1. Refer to the project directions to determine the number and size of the larger squares or rectangles needed for the blocks in your project. Cut out as many background pieces as needed for your project.
2. Refer to the project directions for the number and size of the connector squares needed for your blocks. Cut out as many connector squares as needed for your project.

3. Place a connector square on the appropriate corner of a background square or rectangle with right sides together. Sew diagonally from corner to corner on the connector square, referring to "Sewing Diagonal Lines Accurately" on page 59.

Connector square

4. Trim away the excess fabric, leaving a ¼" seam allowance, as shown; be careful not to trim away the background square or rectangle as you do this.

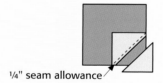

¼" seam allowance

5. Working on the right side of your work, press the connector square toward the corner of the background square or rectangle, creating a triangle shape attached to the background square. Pressing connector squares toward the corner of the background square or rectangle will reduce bulk in the center of the finished block.

Press.

6. Repeat steps 3 through 5 to add connector squares to the blocks needed for your project.

Sewing Diagonal Lines Accurately

Sewing a straight line across the diagonal of a connector square can be a challenge. "Eyeballing" this diagonal line is tricky, particularly if you are working with large connector squares. However, you can mark the diagonal stitching line in one of several ways. For example, you can use a pencil or water-soluble fabric marker and a ruler to draw the diagonal line. You can also press the connector square in half along the diagonal and sew along the crease. (Note that water-soluble pen marks can be heat set with an iron, so be sure to test the pen on a scrap of fabric before using an iron on a marked quilt top.) However, our favorite approach to sewing diagonal lines on connector squares involves marking the machine bed with removable tape, as shown in the following steps.

1. Place an acrylic ruler under the presser foot of your sewing machine, aligning the horizontal lines with the front edge of your sewing-machine bed. This creates an imaginary line that goes from the needle to the front edge of the machine bed.
2. Cut a piece of masking tape or ¼" quilter's tape approximately the same length as the distance from the feed dogs to the front of the machine bed. Place the tape on the machine bed

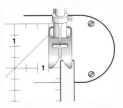

immediately to the right of the ruler. The left edge of the tape should create a straight line that goes from the needle to the front edge of your machine bed.

3. With right sides together, place a connector square on top of the background square or rectangle needed for the block you want to make; line up the corners and the edges of these pieces.
4. Place the connector square underneath the presser foot, so that the needle is positioned exactly at the corner, and the opposite corner is positioned exactly at the left side of the tape.

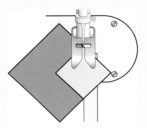

5. Begin sewing just to the right of the corner point on the connector square; this will allow one thread's width of fabric for pressing the seam allowance.

As you sew across the connector square, make sure that both corners stay accurately aligned with the edge of the tape.

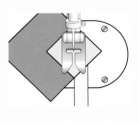

6. Trim away the excess portion of the connector square, leaving a ¼" seam allowance. Be sure not to trim away the background square or rectangle. On the right side of your work, press the connector square toward the corner of the background square or rectangle.

Puss Blocks

1. Refer to the project directions to determine the number of Puss blocks and the size of the rectangles and connector squares required for your project. Cut as many background rectangles and connector squares as you need.
2. Referring to "Using Connector Squares to Create Triangle Shapes" on page 58, sew 2 connector squares to opposite sides of 2 background rectangles. One rectangle should be a mirror image of the other. Press the connector squares toward the corners of the background rectangles.
3. Sew the rectangles together to form a chevron or inverted V shape. Press open the middle seam allowance of the Puss block.

Puss block

Tampa Blocks

1. Refer to the project directions to determine the number of Tampa blocks and the size of the rectangles and connector squares required for your project. Cut as many background rectangles and connector squares as you need.
2. Referring to "Using Connector Squares to Create Triangle Shapes" on page 58, sew 2 large and 2 small connector squares to opposite sides of 2 background rectangles. One rectangle should be a mirror image of the other. Press the connector squares toward the corners of the background rectangles.
3. Sew the rectangles together to form a chevron or inverted V shape. Press the middle seam allowance of the Tampa block open.

Tampa block

Square in a Square Blocks

1. Refer to the project directions to determine the number of Square in a Square blocks and the size of the background squares and connector squares required for your project. Cut as many background squares and connector squares as you need.
2. Referring to "Using Connector Squares to Create Triangle Shapes" on page 58, sew 1 connector square to each corner of the background square. Press the connector squares toward the corners of the background squares.

Square in a Square block

Dugout Blocks

1. Refer to the project directions to determine the number of Dugout blocks and the size of the background squares and connector squares required for your project. Cut as many background squares and connector squares as you need.
2. Referring to "Using Connector Squares to Create Triangle Shapes" on page 58, sew 2 connector squares to opposite corners of the background squares. Press the connector squares toward the corners of the background squares.

Dugout block

Snowball Blocks

1. Refer to the project directions to determine the number of Snowball blocks and the size of the background squares and connector

squares required for your project. Cut as many background squares and connector squares as you need.

2. Referring to "Using Connector Squares to Create Triangle Shapes" on page 58, sew a connector square to each corner of the background square. Press the connector squares toward the corners of the background square.

Snowball block

Hole in the Wall Blocks

1. Refer to the project directions to determine the number of Hole in the Wall blocks needed for your project.

2. Refer to the project cutting chart. Cut the required number of strips and rectangles in the specified widths and colors.

3. Referring to "Rail Blocks" on page 57, sew strip sets and cut segments as specified in the project directions.

4. Sew a rectangle to each side of each segment. Press as needed for your project.

Hole in the
Wall block

Half-Square Triangle Blocks

1. Refer to the project directions to determine the number of Half-Square Triangle blocks and the size of the connector squares required for your project. Cut as many connector squares as you need.

2. Referring to "Using Connector Squares to Create Triangle Shapes" on page 58, sew 2 connector squares together. Trim the excess

fabric, leaving a ¼" seam allowance; press the seam allowance toward the darker of the two fabrics.

Half-Square
Triangle block

Star Points

Add star points to plain blocks or Rail blocks as required by your project.

1. Refer to the project directions to determine the number of Star Points plain blocks or Star Points Rail blocks required for your project. Cut as many plain blocks, Rail strips, and connector squares as you need.

2. If you are making Star Points Rail blocks, sew the Rail blocks as described in "Rail Blocks" on page 57.

3. Referring to "Using Connector Squares to Create Triangle Shapes" on page 58, sew connector squares to 2 or 4 corners of the plain or Rail block as required by your project. Press the connector squares toward the corners of the background block.

Star Points
Rail block

Star Points
plain block

Constructing Design Units

Puss in the Corner and Tampa design units appear in several quilts in this book.

Puss in the Corner Design Units

The Puss in the Corner design unit shown here consists of a nine-patch unit that contains four Four Patch blocks, four Puss blocks, and a plain center block, as shown below. Make the following blocks and arrange on a design wall as shown to make a Puss in the Corner design unit.

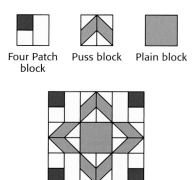

Four Patch   Puss block   Plain block
block

Puss in the Corner
design unit

Tampa Design Units

Tampa design units are much like Puss in the Corner design units, except that one pair of connector squares is only half the size of the other two. Like the Puss in the Corner design unit, the Tampa design unit is a nine patch. It consists of

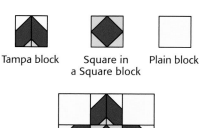

Tampa block   Square in   Plain block
a Square block

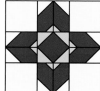

Tampa design unit

the center Square in a Square block, four Tampa blocks, and four plain blocks. Make the blocks and arrange them on a design wall as shown to make a Tampa design unit.

Assembling a Quilt Top with the Four-Patch Method

We also take a systematic approach to sewing all the blocks of a quilt together, sewing small sections into larger ones, and then sewing the larger sections together to create even larger sections until the center of the quilt top is complete. We like this method because it is fast and makes it easier to create a flat quilt top. You are always focused on a matching single "center" seam. You sew pairs of blocks together rather than entire rows or columns, a technique that helps you avoid lumps, bumps, and distortions in the finished quilt top.

1. Start by arranging all of the blocks for your quilt on a design wall in horizontal rows and vertical columns.

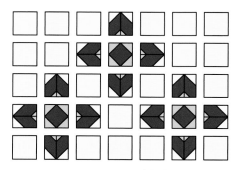

Arrangement of blocks

2. Sew pairs of blocks together to form "two-sies." Press the seam allowances in opposite directions, as indicated by the arrows.

Note: If your project contains an odd number of blocks, add the last one to the final "two-sie" you sew together.

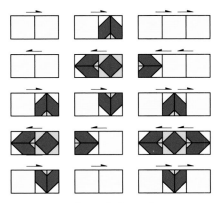

Sew "two-sies" together.
Press.

3. Sew the first pair of blocks to the second pair, as shown. Press these "four-sies" so that all the seam allowances in a column face in the same direction; the seam allowances for the left column should face upward, while the seam allowances for the right column should face downward.

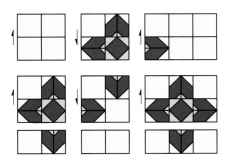

Sew "four-sies" together.
Press.

4. In the same manner, sew the "four-sies" into "eight-sies"; press the seam allowances in opposite direction, as shown by the arrows.

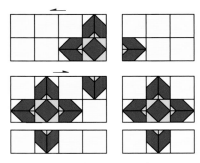

Sew "eight-sies" together.
Press.

5. Continue in the same manner, sewing the "eight-sies" into "sixteen-sies," and so on, until the center of your quilt top is complete (without borders).

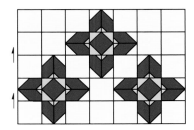

Quilt center complete

Tip You may need to try the four-patch method of assembling a quilt top a time or two before deciding whether it is for you. Be prepared to struggle a bit the first time, because this is not the typical approach taught in beginning quiltmaking classes. By the third time, you should be comfortable with the idea of "two-sies" and "four-sies," and your quilt tops will lie flatter, straighter, and truer than ever before.

Attaching the Borders

The projects in this book feature simple plain or pieced borders. Refer to the project directions for cutting and piecing instructions for your project. You can attach your borders to your quilt with horizontal or vertical corner seams or miter the border corners, as you wish. We suggest that you refer to your favorite basic quilt book for ways to attach borders, or read one of the books we recommend in "Bibliography" on page 96. Whichever method you choose for attaching the borders to your quilt, take time to measure the width and length of your completed quilt top through the center in both directions to determine the most accurate measurements for your borders.

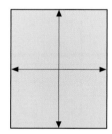

Measure center of
quilt in both directions.

Layering and Basting

A quilt sandwich consists of three layers: the backing, the batting, and the quilt top. To make the backing for any of the projects in this book, measure the length and width of your finished quilt top after you attach the borders. Add 4" to each of these measurements, and cut or piece a backing that size for your quilt. Then follow these steps to layer and baste the quilt sandwich to prepare it for hand or machine quilting.

1. Place the quilt backing, wrong side up, on a flat surface like a table or floor, using masking tape to anchor it in place.

2. Position the batting on top of the backing, smoothing out any wrinkles.
3. Center your completed quilt top, right side up, over the batting, smoothing out any wrinkles and making sure that the edges lie parallel to the edges of the backing.
4. Baste the 3 layers of the quilt sandwich together with 1" rustproof safety pins. Place pins 3" to 4" apart, avoiding areas where you plan to quilt.

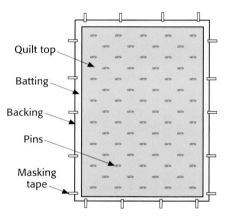

Quilt top
Batting
Backing
Pins
Masking tape

Tip Open up the batting for your quilt and spread it out on a flat surface overnight to allow the fibers to "relax" before you layer the quilt sandwich.

Hand or Machine Quilting

For instructions on hand quilting techniques, we recommend the book *Loving Stitches* by Jeana Kimball; for machine quilting instructions, we suggest *Machine Quilting Made Easy* by Maurine Noble (see "Bibliography" on page 96).

Attaching the Binding

To make double-fold French binding for the projects in this book, you will need to measure the distance around the edges of your quilt and add 10" extra to allow for mitering a fold at each corner. Cut as many 2¼" x 42" (width of the fabric) straight-grain binding strips as it takes to reach this measurement and follow these steps to attach the binding to your quilt.

1. Trim the batting and backing even with the edges of the quilt top.
2. Join the binding strips, right sides together, with diagonal seams to make one long piece of binding. Trim the seam allowances to ¼" and press them open.

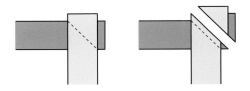

3. Fold the binding in half lengthwise, with wrong sides together, and press.
4. Leaving the first 10" to 12" of binding free and starting away from a corner of the quilt, stitch the binding to the quilt using a ¼" seam allowance. Stop stitching exactly ¼" from the corner of the quilt and backstitch. Clip the thread.

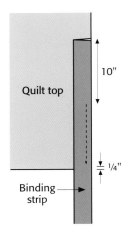

5. Fold the binding up and away from the quilt; then fold the binding back down on itself, forming a fold that is parallel with the edge of the quilt top. Beginning at the point where your previous line of stitching ended, stitch the binding to this side of the quilt.

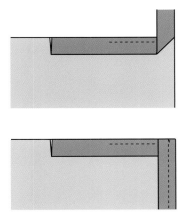

6. Continue stitching the binding to each side of the quilt in the same way, folding the binding up and back down on itself in the same manner at each corner.
7. When you reach 10" from your starting point, stop stitching and remove the quilt from the sewing machine. Lay the quilt on a flat surface. Fold the unsewn binding ends back on themselves, so that they just meet in the middle over the unstitched area of the quilt. Finger-press both binding strips to mark where they meet each other.

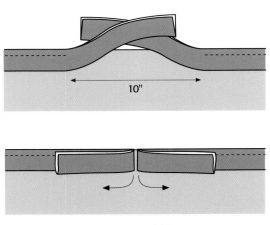

Finger-press folds.

8. Unfold the bindings and match the center of the pressed Xs. Sew across the intersection diagonally. Trim the excess fabric, leaving a ¼" seam allowance; finger-press this seam allowance open.

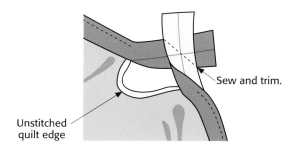

Sew and trim.

Unstitched quilt edge

9. Fold the binding in half again and finish stitching it to the quilt.

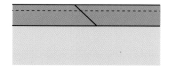

10. Fold the binding over the raw edges to the back side of the quilt. Blindstitch the binding to the quilt backing with the folded edge covering the machine stitching. A miter will form at each corner; blindstitch these folds in place.

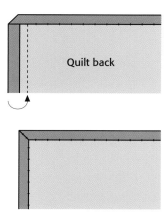

Quilt back

Adding a Label

Remember to add a label to the lower right side of your quilt backing. Include your name as the quiltmaker, the date you finished the quilt, and the name of the recipient if the quilt is to be a gift. You can write this information on a piece of muslin with a permanent fabric-marking pen. Fold the edges under and blindstitch the label in place.

Puss in the Corner

Block Size: 4"
Finished Quilt: 50" x 62"

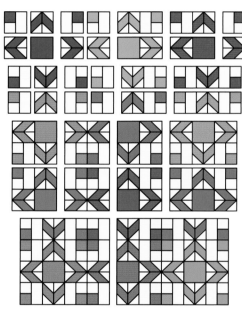

Fabric Yardage

3 yds. background
(including binding)
12 fat quarters colorful prints
3¼ yds. backing

Design Unit

Puss in the Corner

Blocks You'll Need

48 Puss blocks

48 Four Patch blocks

12 plain blocks

CUTTING Cut strips across fabric width.

FABRIC	BLOCK/ BORDER	No. of STRIPS	STRIP WIDTH	ADDITIONAL CUTTING INSTRUCTIONS
Background	Four Patch	3	2½"	Cut 48 squares, each 2½" x 2½".
		3	4½"	Cut 48 rectangles, each 2½" x 4½".
	Puss	12	2½"	Cut 192 squares, each 2½" x 2½".
	Inner Border	5	1½"	Measure quilt top and cut border strips to fit.
	Outer Border	6	4½"	Measure quilt top and cut border strips to fit.
Colorful Prints	Four Patch			Cut 4 squares, each 2½" x 2½", from each fat quarter.
	Puss			Cut 8 rectangles, each 2½" x 4½", from each fat quarter.
	Plain			Cut 1 square, 4½" x 4½", from each fat quarter.
	Pieced Border			Cut approximately 3 strips from each fat quarter, 22" long and in random widths from 1" to 2"; cut strips into rectangles, 2½" on the long side. Sew short ends of rectangles together randomly as needed for each side of quilt.

Sewing

1. Referring to the quilt photo on page 68, "Plain Blocks" on page 56, "Four Patch Blocks" on page 56, "Puss Blocks" on page 60, and the cutting chart, cut and assemble all required blocks. Place the blocks on a design wall.

2. Refer to "Assembling a Quilt Top with the Four-Patch Method" on page 62 to complete the quilt center.

3. Add the inner border, the pieced border, and the outer border, referring to the quilt photo and the cutting chart.

4. Refer to "Layering and Basting" on page 64 to prepare the quilt sandwich for quilting.

5. Quilt by hand or machine, as desired.

6. Refer to "Attaching the Binding" on page 65 and "Adding a Label" on page 66 to complete the quilt.

Plain Jane Pusses

Block size: 3"
Finished Quilt: 45" x 57"

Fabric Yardage

2¾ yds. background
   (including binding)
12 fat quarters colorful prints
3¼ yds. backing
Note: Quilt contains 18 Puss in the Corner design units; use some colorful prints in more than one design unit, as desired.

Design Unit

Puss in the Corner

Blocks You'll Need

72 Puss blocks

18 colorful plain blocks

75 background plain blocks

CUTTING Cut strips across fabric width.

FABRIC	BLOCK/BORDER	No. of STRIPS	STRIP WIDTH	ADDITIONAL CUTTING INSTRUCTIONS
Background	Plain	7	3½"	Cut 75 squares, each 3½" x 3½".
	Puss	15	2"	Cut 288 squares, each 2" x 2".
	Inner Border	4	1½"	Measure quilt top and cut border strips to fit.
	Outer Border	5	3½"	Measure quilt top and cut border strips to fit.
Colorful Prints	Plain			Cut one 3½" square for each Puss in the Corner design unit.
	Puss			Cut 8 rectangles, each 2" x 3½", for each Puss in the Corner design unit.
	Pieced Border			Cut a total of 63 rectangles, each 2" x 3½", from fat quarters; sew short ends of rectangles together randomly as needed for each side of quilt.

Sewing

1. Referring to the quilt photo on page 70, "Plain Blocks" on page 56, "Puss Blocks" on page 60, and the cutting chart, cut and assemble all required blocks. Group the blocks on a design wall.
2. Refer to "Assembling a Quilt Top with the Four-Patch Method" on page 62 to complete the quilt center.
3. Add the inner border, the pieced border, and the outer border, referring to the quilt photo and the cutting chart.
4. Refer to "Layering and Basting" on page 64 to prepare the quilt sandwich for quilting.
5. Quilt by hand or machine, as desired.
6. Refer to "Attaching the Binding" on page 65 and "Adding a Label" on page 66 to complete the quilt.

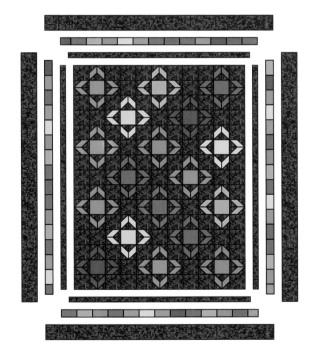

Star-Studded Gecko Pusses

Block size: 3"
Finished Quilt: 39" x 51"

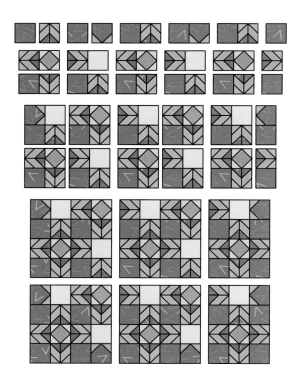

Fabric Yardage

2¼ yds. background
   (including binding)
⅓ yd. red
⅓ yd. gold
1 yd. orange
⅓ yd. light lime green
⅝ yd. medium lime green
2¾ yds. backing

Design Unit

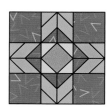

Puss in the Corner

Blocks You'll Need

 72 Puss blocks

 18 Square in
a Square blocks

 10 Star Points
plain blocks

 17 lime green
plain blocks

 48 background
plain blocks

CUTTING Cut strips across fabric width.

FABRIC	BLOCK/ BORDER	No. of STRIPS	STRIP WIDTH	ADDITIONAL CUTTING INSTRUCTIONS
Background	Plain	5	3½"	Cut 48 squares, each 3½" x 3½".
	Puss	8	2"	Cut 144 squares, each 2" x 2".
	SPP**	1	3½"	Cut 10 squares, each 3½" x 3½".
	Border	5	3"	Measure quilt top and cut border strips to fit.
Red	SnS*	2	3½"	Cut 18 squares, each 3½" x 3½".
Gold	SnS*	4	2"	Cut 72 squares, each 2" x 2".
Orange	Puss	8	3½"	Cut 144 rectangles, each 2" x 3½".
Light Lime Green	Plain	2	3½"	Cut 17 squares, each 3½" x 3½".
Medium Lime Green	Puss	8	2"	Cut 144 squares, each 2" x 2".
	SPP**	1	2"	Cut 20 squares, each 2" x 2".

* Square in a Square, **Star Points Plain

Sewing

1. Referring to the quilt photo on page 72, "Plain Blocks" on page 56, "Puss Blocks" on page 60, "Square in a Square Blocks" on page 60, "Star Points" on page 61, and the cutting chart, cut and assemble all required blocks. Group the blocks on a design wall.

2. Refer to "Assembling a Quilt Top with the Four-Patch Method" on page 62 to complete the quilt center.

3. Add the border, referring to the quilt photo and the cutting chart.

4. Refer to "Layering and Basting" on page 64 to prepare the quilt sandwich for quilting.

5. Quilt by hand or machine, as desired.

6. Refer to "Attaching the Binding" on page 65 and "Adding a Label" on page 66 to complete the quilt.

Pretty Tampas All in a Row

Block Size: 3"
Finished Quilt: 40" x 49"

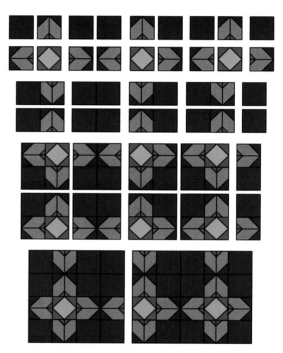

Fabric Yardage

2¼ yds. background
   (including binding)
⅞ yd. red
½ yd. dark blue
½ yd. light blue
2¾ yds. backing

Design Unit

Tampa

Blocks You'll Need

48 Tampa blocks

12 Square in a Square blocks

48 background plain blocks

CUTTING Cut strips across fabric width.

FABRIC	BLOCK/ BORDER	# STRIPS	STRIP WIDTH	ADDITIONAL CUTTING INSTRUCTIONS
Background	Plain	5	3½"	Cut 48 squares, each 3½" x 3½".
	Tampa	5	2"	Cut 96 squares, each 2" x 2".
	Inner Border	4	1½"	Measure quilt top and cut border strips to fit.
	Outer Border	5	4"	Measure quilt top and cut border strips to fit.
Red	Tampa	5	3½"	Cut 96 rectangles, each 2" x 3½".
	Pieced Border	5		*Cut strips in random widths. Sew strips into random strip sets with corresponding light blue strips; cut into 1½" segments. Measure quilt top and cut border strips to fit.
Dark Blue	SnS**	3	2"	Cut 48 squares, each 2" x 2".
	Tampa	2	1¼"	Cut 96 squares, each 1¼" x 1¼".
Light Blue	SnS**	2	3½"	Cut 12 squares, each 3½" x 3½".
	Pieced Border	5		See * above.

**Square in a Square

Sewing

1. Referring to the quilt photo on page 74, "Plain Blocks" on page 56, "Tampa Blocks" on page 60, "Square in a Square Blocks" on page 60, and the cutting chart, make and assemble all required blocks. Group the blocks on a design wall.

2. Refer to "Assembling a Quilt Top with the Four-Patch Method" on page 62 to complete the quilt center.

3. Add the inner border, the pieced border, and the outer border, referring to the quilt photo and the cutting chart.

4. Refer to "Layering and Basting" on page 64 to prepare the quilt sandwich for quilting.

5. Quilt by hand or machine, as desired.

6. Refer to "Attaching the Binding" on page 65 and "Adding a Label" on page 66 to complete the quilt.

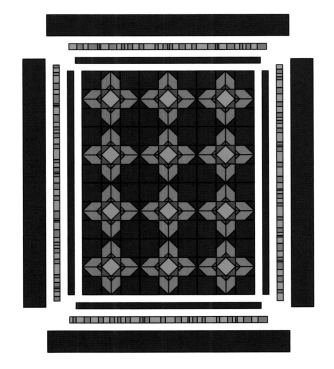

SnS Tampas

Block Size: 4"
Finished Quilt: 46½" x 58½"

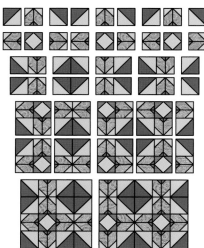

Fabric Yardage

2¼ yds. fall "swirlies"
    (including binding)
1½ yds. dark green
1⅜ yds. light green
⅓ yd. gold
½ yd. rust
3¼ yds. backing

Design Unit

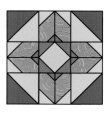

Tampa

Blocks You'll Need

48 Tampa blocks

12 Square in a
Square blocks

48 Half-Square
Triangle blocks

CUTTING Cut strips across fabric width.

FABRIC	BLOCK/ BORDER	No. of STRIPS	STRIP WIDTH	ADDITIONAL CUTTING INSTRUCTIONS
Fall "Swirlies"	Tampa	6	4½"	Cut 96 rectangles, each 2½" x 4½".
	Outer Border	5	4½"	Measure quilt top and cut border strips to fit.
Dark Green	Half-Square Triangle	6	4½"	Cut 48 squares, each 4½" x 4½".
	Inner Border	5	1¾"	Measure quilt top and cut border strips to fit.
Light Green	Half-Square Triangle	6	4½"	Cut 48 squares, each 4½" x 4½".
	Tampa	6	2½"	Cut 96 squares, each 2½" x 2½".
Gold	SnS*	2	4½"	Cut 12 squares, each 4½" x 4½".
Rust	SnS*	3	2½"	Cut 48 squares, each 2½" x 2½".
	Tampa	4	1½"	Cut 96 squares, each 1½" x 1½".

*Square in a Square

Sewing

1. Referring to the quilt photo on page 76, "Tampa Blocks" on page 60, "Square in a Square Blocks" on page 60, and "Half-Square Triangle Blocks" on page 61, and the cutting chart, cut and assemble all required blocks. Group the blocks on a design wall.

2. Refer to "Assembling a Quilt Top with the Four-Patch Method" on page 62 to complete the quilt center.

3. Add the inner border and the outer border, referring to the quilt photo and the cutting chart.

4. Refer to "Layering and Basting" on page 64 to prepare the quilt sandwich for quilting.

5. Quilt by hand or machine, as desired.

6. Refer to "Attaching the Binding" on page 65 and "Adding a Label" on page 66 to complete the quilt.

Tampa Waterlilies

Block Size: 3"
Finished Quilt: 35" x 44"

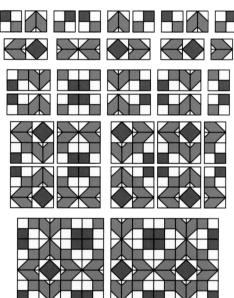

Fabric Yardage

1¼ yds. background
⅞ yd. purple
½ yd. green
1 yd. border print
   (including binding)
1¾ yds. backing

Design Unit

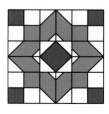

Tampa

Blocks You'll Need

48 Tampa blocks

12 Square in a
Square blocks

48 Four Patch blocks

CUTTING Cut strips across fabric width.

FABRIC	BLOCK/ BORDER	No. of STRIPS	STRIP WIDTH	ADDITIONAL CUTTING INSTRUCTIONS
Background	Tampa	5	2"	Cut 96 squares, each 2" x 2".
	Tampa	3	1¼"	Cut 96 squares, each 1¼" x 1¼".
	SnS**	3	2"	Cut 48 squares, each 2" x 2".
	Four Patch	6	2"	*Make 6 strip sets, 3 background and purple and 3 background and green; cut 48 segments, each 2" long, from each color combination.
	Inner Border	4	1¼"	Measure quilt top and cut border strips to fit.
Purple	Tampa	5	3½"	Cut 96 rectangles, each 2" x 3½".
	Four Patch	3	2"	See * above.
Green	SnS**	1	3½"	Cut 12 squares, each 3½" x 3½".
	Four Patch	3	2"	See * above.
Border Print	Outer Border	4	4½"	Measure quilt top and cut border strips to fit.

**Square in a Square

Sewing

1. Referring to the quilt photo on page 78, "Four Patch Blocks" on page 56, "Tampa Blocks" on page 60, "Square in a Square Blocks" on page 60, and the cutting chart, cut and assemble all required blocks. Group the blocks on a design wall.

2. Refer to "Assembling a Quilt Top with the Four-Patch Method" on page 62 to complete the quilt center.

3. Add the inner border and the outer border, referring to the quilt photo and the cutting chart.

4. Refer to "Layering and Basting" on page 64 to prepare the quilt sandwich for quilting.

5. Quilt by hand or machine, as desired.

6. Refer to "Attaching the Binding" on page 65 and "Adding a Label" on page 66 to complete the quilt.

Pretty Tampa Trellis II

Block Size: 4"
Finished Quilt: 46" x 58"

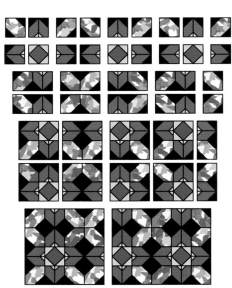

Fabric Yardage

2¼ yds. floral
   (including binding)
1¼ yds. black
1 yd. fuchsia
⅓ yd. blue
½ yd. gold
3 yds. backing

Design Unit

Tampa

Blocks You'll Need

 48 Tampa blocks

 12 Square in a
Square blocks

 48 Dugout blocks

CUTTING Cut strips across fabric width.

FABRIC	BLOCK/ BORDER	No. of STRIPS	STRIP WIDTH	ADDITIONAL CUTTING INSTRUCTIONS
Floral	Dugout	6	4½"	Cut 48 squares, each 4½" x 4½".
	Outer Border	5	4½"	Measure quilt top and cut border strips to fit.
Black	Tampa	6	2½"	Cut 96 squares, each 2½" x 2½".
	Dugout	6	2½"	Cut 96 squares, each 2½" x 2½".
	Inner Border	5	1½"	Measure quilt top and cut border strips to fit.
Fuchsia	Tampa	6	4½"	Cut 96 rectangles, each 2½" x 4½".
Blue	SnS*	2	4½"	Cut 12 squares, each 4½" x 4½".
Gold	SnS*	3	2½"	Cut 48 squares, each 2½" x 2½".
	Tampa	4	1½"	Cut 96 squares, each 1½" x 1½".

*Square in a Square

Sewing

1. Referring to the quilt photo on page 80, "Tampa Blocks" on page 60, "Square in a Square Blocks" on page 60, "Dugout Blocks" on page 60, and the cutting chart, cut and assemble all required blocks. Group the design units on a design wall.

2. Refer to "Assembling a Quilt Top with the Four-Patch Method" on page 62 to complete the quilt center.

3. Add the inner border and the outer border, referring to the quilt photo and the cutting chart.

4. Refer to "Layering and Basting" on page 64 to prepare the quilt sandwich for quilting.

5. Quilt by hand or machine, as desired.

6. Refer to "Attaching the Binding" on page 65 and "Adding a Label" on page 66 to complete the quilt.

Original Tampa Connects Up

Block Size: 3"
Finished Quilt: 39" x 51"

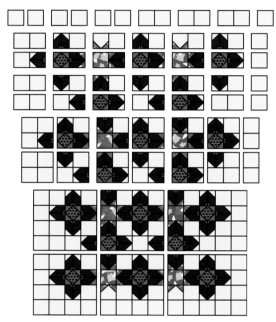

Fabric Yardage

1¾ yds. background
1¼ yds. dark blue
   (including binding)
⅓ yd. medium blue
⅝ yd. dark red
⅝ yd. medium red
2¾ yds. backing

Design Unit

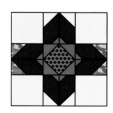

Tampa

Blocks You'll Need

44 Tampa blocks
with background

28 Tampa blocks
with medium red

18 Square in a
Square blocks

4 Star Points
plain blocks

119 background
plain blocks

8 medium red
plain blocks

CUTTING Cut strips across fabric width.

FABRIC	BLOCK	No. of STRIPS	STRIP WIDTH	ADDITIONAL CUTTING INSTRUCTIONS
Background	Plain	11	3½"	Cut 119 squares, each 3½" x 3½".
	Star Points Plain	1	3½"	Cut 4 squares, each 3½" x 3½".
	Tampa	5	2"	Cut 88 squares, each 2" x 2".
Dark Blue	Tampa	8	3½"	Cut 144 rectangles, each 2" x 3½".
Medium Blue	SnS*	2	3½"	Cut 18 squares, each 3½" x 3½".
Dark Red	Tampa	5	1¼"	Cut 144 squares, each 1¼" x 1¼".
	SnS*	4	2"	Cut 72 squares, each 2" x 2".
Medium Red	Tampa (Red)	3	2"	Cut 56 squares, each 2" x 2".
	Star Points Plain	1	2"	Cut 8 squares, each 2" x 2".
	Plain	1	3½"	Cut 8 squares, each 3½" x 3½".

*Square in a Square

Sewing

1. Referring to the quilt photo on page 82, "Plain Blocks" on page 56, "Tampa Blocks" on page 60, "Square in a Square Blocks" on page 60, "Star Points" on page 61, and the cutting chart, cut and assemble all required blocks. Group the blocks on a design wall.

2. Refer to "Assembling a Quilt Top with the Four-Patch Method" on page 62 to complete the quilt center.

3. Refer to "Layering and Basting" on page 64 to prepare the quilt sandwich for quilting.

4. Quilt by hand or machine, as desired.

5. Refer to "Attaching the Binding" on page 65 and "Adding a Label" on page 66 to complete the quilt.

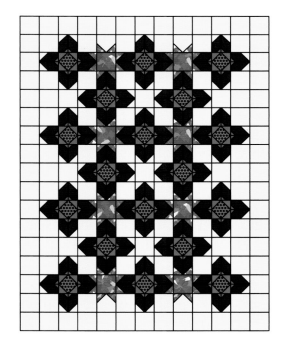

Tampas Go Hawaiian

Block Size: 3"
Finished Quilt: 45" x 45"

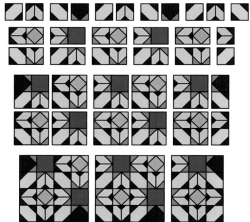

Fabric Yardage

Note: The pictured quilt features several different values of cheddar, purple, and fuchsia. If you want to use different values in your quilt, choose assorted fabrics totaling the yardage amounts given below.

1 yd. cheddar
¼ yd. dark turquoise
½ yd. medium turquoise
⅝ yd. light turquoise
1 yd. dark purple
¼ yd. purple
⅓ yd. fuchsia
1¼ yds. Hawaiian print (including binding)
3 yds. backing

Design Unit

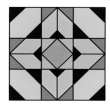

Tampa

Blocks You'll Need

 40 Tampa blocks with medium turquoise

 12 Tampa blocks with dark purple

 13 Square in a Square blocks

 36 Dugout blocks

 8 Star Points plain blocks

 12 dark turquoise plain blocks

FABRIC	BLOCK/ BORDER	No. of STRIPS	STRIP WIDTH	ADDITIONAL CUTTING INSTRUCTIONS
CUTTING Cut strips across fabric width.				
Cheddar	Tampa	6	3½"	Cut 104 rectangles, each 2" x 3½".
Dark Turquoise	Plain	2	3½"	Cut 12 squares, each 3½" x 3½".
Medium Turquoise	Tampa	4	2"	Cut 80 squares, each 2" x 2".
	Star Points Plain	1	2"	Cut 16 squares, each 2" x 2".
Light Turquoise	Dugout	4	3½"	Cut 36 squares, each 3½" x 3½".
Dark Purple	Tampa	4	1¼"	Cut 104 squares, each 1¼" x 1¼".
	Tampa	2	2"	Cut 24 squares, each 2" x 2".
	Star Points Plain	1	3½"	Cut 8 squares, each 3½" x 3½".
	Inner Border	4	1¾"	Measure quilt top and cut border strips to fit.
Purple	SnS*	3	2"	Cut 52 squares, each 2" x 2".
	Pieced Border	1	random width between 1" and 2"	*Make 1 purple-and-fuchsia strip set. Cut number of 1½" segments required for border (based on quilt-top measurement); join segments to create border.
Fuchsia	SnS*	2	3½"	Cut 13 squares, each 3½" x 3½".
	Pieced Border	1	random width between 1" and 2"	See * above.
Hawaiian Print	Outer Border	5	5½"	Measure quilt top and cut border strips to fit.

*Square in a Square

Sewing

1. Referring to the quilt photo on page 84, "Plain Blocks" on page 56, "Tampa Blocks" on page 60, "Square in a Square Blocks" on page 60, "Dugout Blocks" on page 60, "Star Points" on page 61, and the cutting chart, cut and assemble all required blocks. Group the blocks on a design wall.

2. Refer to "Assembling a Quilt Top with the Four-Patch Method" on page 62 to complete the quilt center.

3. Add the inner border, pieced border, and outer border, referring to the quilt photo and the cutting chart.

4. Refer to "Layering and Basting" on page 64 to prepare the quilt sandwich for quilting.

5. Quilt by hand or machine, as desired.

6. Refer to "Attaching the Binding" on page 65 and "Adding a Label" on page 66 to complete the quilt.

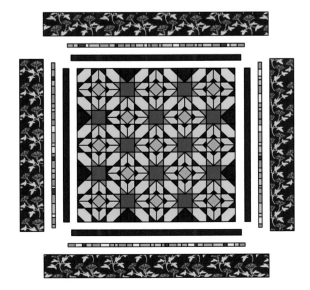

Tampa Christmas Poinsettias

Block Size: 3"
Finished Quilt: 45" x 45"

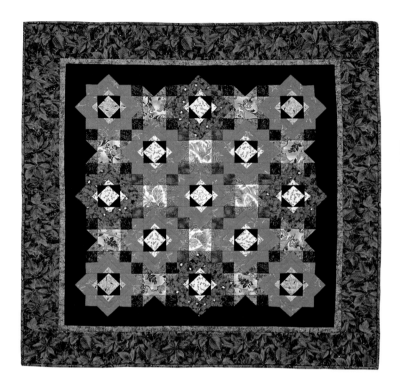

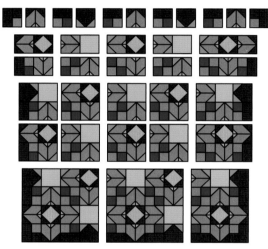

Fabric Yardage

½ yd. cream
1 yd. red
1 yd. black
⅓ yd. light green
½ yd. medium green
¼ yd. dark green
1¼ yds. poinsettia print (including binding)
3 yds. backing

Design Unit

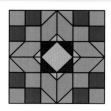

Tampa

Blocks You'll Need

 40 Tampa blocks with green

 12 Tampa blocks with black

 13 Square in a Square blocks

 8 Star Points plain blocks

16 Four Patch blocks

 2 Four Patch blocks (red on top)

 2 Four Patch blocks (red on bottom)

 8 Four Patch blocks (red on top)

 8 Four Patch blocks (red on bottom)

 12 light green plain blocks

CUTTING Cut strips across fabric width.

FABRIC	BLOCK/ BORDER	No. of STRIPS	STRIP WIDTH	ADDITIONAL CUTTING INSTRUCTIONS
Cream	SnS*	2	3½"	Cut 13 squares, each 3½" x 3½".
	Tampa	4	1¼"	Cut 104 squares, each 1¼" x 1¼".
Red	Tampa	6	3½"	Cut 104 rectangles, each 2" x 3½".
	Four Patch	3	2"	**Make 3 strip sets, 2 red and green and 1 black and red. Cut black-and-red strip set into 4 segments, each 2" long. Cut red-and-green strip sets into 48 segments, each 2" long.
Black	Star Points	1	3½"	Cut 8 squares, each 3½" x 3½".
	Tampa	2	2"	Cut 24 squares, each 2" x 2".
	Four Patch	1	2"	See ** above.
	Four Patch	1	3½"	Cut 20 rectangles, each 2" x 3½".
	Inner Border	4	1¾"	Measure quilt top and cut border strips to fit.
Light Green	Plain	1	3½"	Cut 12 squares, each 3½" x 3½".
	Middle Border	4	1¼"	Measure quilt top and cut border strips to fit.
Medium Green	Star Points Plain	1	2"	Cut 16 squares, each 2" x 2".
	Tampa	6	2"	Cut 80 squares, each 2" x 2".
Dark Green	Four Patch	2	2"	See ** above.
Poinsettia	Outer Border	5	5"	Measure quilt top and cut border strips to fit.

*Square in a Square

Sewing

1. Referring to the quilt photo on page 86, "Plain Blocks" on page 56, "Four Patch Blocks" on page 56, "Tampa Blocks" on page 60, "Square in a Square Blocks" on page 60, "Star Points" on page 61, and the cutting chart, cut and assemble all required blocks. Group the blocks on a design wall.

2. Refer to "Assembling a Quilt Top with the Four-Patch Method" on page 62 to complete the quilt center.

3. Add the inner border, middle border, and outer border, referring to the quilt photo and the cutting chart.

4. Refer to "Layering and Basting" on page 64 to prepare the quilt sandwich for quilting.

5. Quilt by hand or machine, as desired.

6. Refer to "Attaching the Binding" on page 65 and "Adding a Label" on page 66 to complete the quilt.

Bugs!

Block Sizes: 2¼" and 5½"
Finished Quilt: 60" x 68"

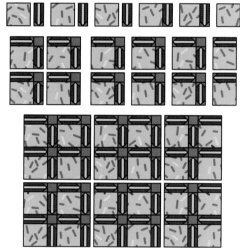

Fabric Yardage

3 yds. bug print
  (including binding)
1¼ yds. red
1½ yds. black print
⅝ yd. green
3¾ yds. backing

Design Unit

Four Patch Star

Blocks You'll Need

 49 Star Points Rail blocks
(with points on 2 ends)

 22 Star Points Rail blocks

 30 red plain blocks

 42 bug-print plain blocks

CUTTING Cut strips across fabric width.

FABRIC	BLOCK/ BORDER	# STRIPS	STRIP WIDTH	ADDITIONAL CUTTING INSTRUCTIONS
Bugs	Plain	7	6"	Cut 42 squares, each 6" x 6".
	Outer Border	6	7"	Measure quilt top and cut border strips to fit.
Red	Plain	3	2¾"	Cut 30 squares, each 2¾" x 2¾".
	Star Points Rail	11	1¾"	Cut 240 squares, each 1¾" x 1¾".
	Middle Border	5	⅞"	Measure quilt top and cut border strips to fit.
Black	Star Points Rail	24	1¼"	*Make 12 black-green-black strip sets; cut into 71 segments, each 6" long.
	Inner Border	5	⅞"	Measure quilt top and cut border strips to fit.
Green	Star Points Rail	12	1¼"	See * above.

Sewing

1. Referring to the quilt photo on page 88, "Plain Blocks" on page 56, "Star Points" on page 61, and the cutting chart, cut and assemble all required blocks. Group the blocks on a design wall.

Note: The Star Points edges do not match exactly to the edges of the red plain blocks. They are about ¼" from the seam line.

2. Refer to "Assembling a Quilt Top with the Four-Patch Method" on page 62 to complete the quilt center.

3. Add the inner border, middle border, and outer border, referring to the quilt photo and the cutting chart.

4. Refer to "Layering and Basting" on page 64 to prepare the quilt sandwich for quilting.

5. Quilt by hand or machine, as desired.

6. Refer to "Attaching the Binding" on page 65 and "Adding a Label" on page 66 to complete the quilt.

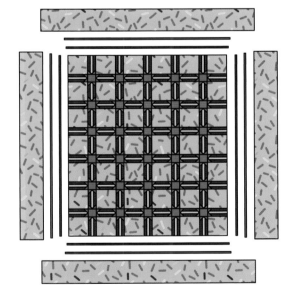

Circus Tents

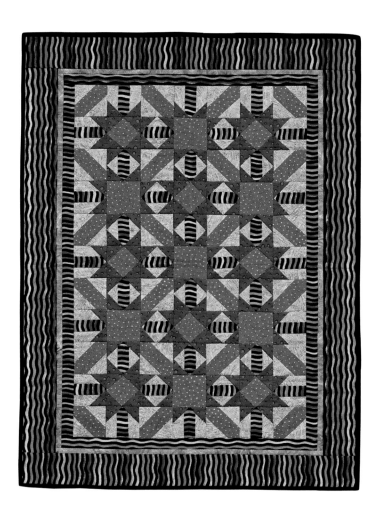

Block Size: 3"
Finished Quilt: 33" x 45"

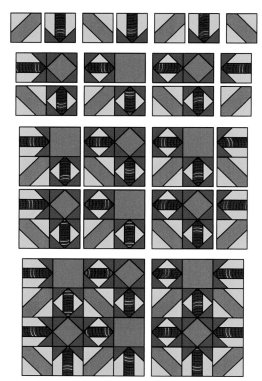

Fabric Yardage

¾ yd. cheddar
¾ yd. red
⅝ yd. blue
1½ yds. multicolor stripe
  (including binding)
¼ yd. yellow-green
1½ yds. backing

Design Unit

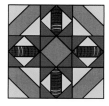

Design unit

Blocks You'll Need

 8 Square in a Square blocks

 22 Star Points Rail blocks (with points on two ends)

 16 Star Points Rail blocks

 24 Dugout blocks

 7 plain blocks

CUTTING **Cut strips across fabric width.**

FABRIC	BLOCK	# STRIPS	STRIP WIDTH	ADDITIONAL CUTTING INSTRUCTIONS
Cheddar	Dugout	3	2"	Cut 48 squares, each 2" x 2".
	Star Points Rail	8	1½"	*Make 4 cheddar-multicolored-cheddar strip sets; cut into 38 segments, each 3½" long.
Red	Plain	1	3½"	Cut 7 squares, each 3½" x 3½".
	Dugout	3	3½"	Cut 24 squares, each 3½" x 3½".
	SnS**	1	3½"	Cut 8 squares, each 3½" x 3½".
Blue	SnS**	2	2"	Cut 32 squares, each 2" x 2".
	Star Points Rail	6	2"	Cut 120 squares, each 2" x 2".
Multicolor Stripe	Star Points Rail	4	1½"	See * above.
	Inner Border	4	½"	Measure quilt top and cut border strips to fit.
	Outer Border	4	3½"	Measure quilt top and cut border strips to fit.
Yellow-Green	Middle Border	4	1"	Measure quilt top and cut border strips to fit.

**Square in a Square

Sewing

1. Referring to the quilt photo on page 90, "Plain Blocks" on page 56, "Square in a Square Blocks" on page 60, "Dugout Blocks" on page 60, "Star Points" on page 61, and the cutting chart, cut and assemble all required blocks. Group the blocks on a design wall.

2. Refer to "Assembling a Quilt Top with the Four-Patch Method" on page 62 to complete the quilt center.

3. Add the inner border, middle border, and outer border, referring to the quilt photo and the cutting chart.

4. Refer to "Layering and Basting" on page 64 to prepare the quilt sandwich for quilting.

5. Quilt by hand or machine, as desired.

6. Refer to "Attaching the Binding" on page 65 and "Adding a Label" on page 66 to complete the quilt.

Floral Tents

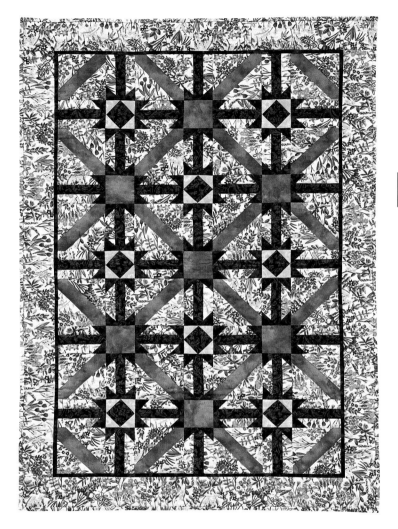

Block Sizes: 3" and 5"
Finished Quilt: 39" x 55"

Fabric Yardage

2½ yds. floral background
   (including binding)
1 yd. pink
½ yd. green
¾ yd. purple
¼ yd. yellow
2¾ yds. backing

Design Unit

Four Patch Star

Blocks You'll Need

 8 Square in a
Square blocks

 22 Star Points Rail blocks
(with points on 2 ends)

 16 Star Points Rail blocks
(with points on 1 end)

 24 Dugout blocks

 7 plain blocks

CUTTING **Cut strips across fabric width.**

FABRIC	BLOCK	# STRIPS	STRIP WIDTH	ADDITIONAL CUTTING INSTRUCTIONS
Floral Background	Dugout	6	$4\frac{1}{2}$"	Cut 48 squares, each $4\frac{1}{2}$" x $4\frac{1}{2}$".
	Star Points Rail	12	$1\frac{1}{2}$"	*Make 6 background-green-background strip sets; cut into 38 rectangles, each $3\frac{1}{2}$" x $5\frac{1}{2}$".
	Outer Border	5	$3\frac{1}{2}$"	Measure quilt top and cut border strips to fit.
Pink	Plain	1	$3\frac{1}{2}$"	Cut 7 squares, each $3\frac{1}{2}$" x $3\frac{1}{2}$".
	Dugout	4	$5\frac{1}{2}$"	Cut 24 squares, each $5\frac{1}{2}$" x $5\frac{1}{2}$".
Green	SnS**	1	$3\frac{1}{2}$"	Cut 8 squares, each $3\frac{1}{2}$" x $3\frac{1}{2}$".
	Star Points Rail	6	$1\frac{1}{2}$"	See * above.
Purple	Star Points Rail	6	2"	Cut 120 squares, each 2" x 2".
	Inner Border	4	1"	Measure quilt top and cut border strips to fit.
Yellow	SnS**	2	2"	Cut 32 squares, each 2" x 2".

**Square in a Square

Sewing

1. Referring to the quilt photo on page 92, "Plain Blocks" on page 56, "Square in a Square Blocks" on page 60, "Dugout Blocks" on page 60, "Star Points" on page 61, and the cutting chart, cut and assemble all required blocks. Group the blocks on a design wall.

2. Refer to "Assembling a Quilt Top with the Four-Patch Method" on page 62 to complete the quilt center.

3. Add inner border and outer border, referring to the quilt photo and the cutting chart.

4. Refer to "Layering and Basting" on page 64 to prepare the quilt sandwich for quilting.

5. Quilt by hand or machine, as desired.

6. Refer to "Attaching the Binding" on page 65 and "Adding a Label" on page 66 to complete the quilt.

Turquoise Tango

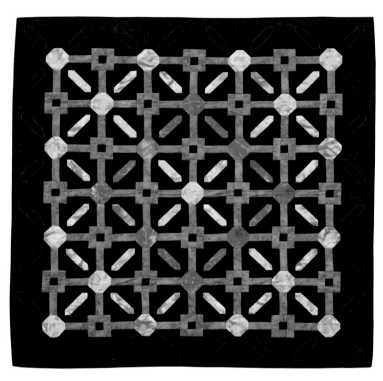

Block Size: 3"
Finished Quilt: 47" x 47"

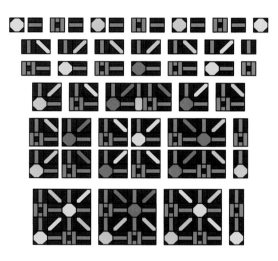

Fabric Yardage

2½ yds. black background
(including binding)
½ yd. red
½ yd. gold
½ yd. green
⅞ yd. turquoise
3¼ yds. backing

Design Unit

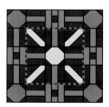

Four Patch Star

Blocks You'll Need

 8 green
Snowball blocks

 9 gold
Snowball blocks

 8 red
Snowball blocks

 16 green
Dugout blocks

 12 gold
Dugout blocks

 8 red
Dugout blocks

 24 Hole in the
Wall blocks

 84 Rail blocks

CUTTING **Cut strips across fabric width.**

FABRIC	BLOCK	# STRIPS	STRIP WIDTH	ADDITIONAL CUTTING INSTRUCTIONS
Black Background	Rail	16	1½"	*Make 8 black-turquoise-black strip sets; cut into 84 squares, each 3½" x 3½".
	Hole in the Wall	2	1½"	**Make 2 turquoise-black-turquoise strip sets; cut into 24 segments, each 1½" x 3½".
	Dugout	5	2¾"	Cut 72 squares, each 2¾" x 2¾".
	Snowball	4	1½"	Cut 100 squares, each 1½" x 1½".
	Border	5	4½"	Measure quilt top and cut border strips to fit.
Red	Snowball	1	3½"	Cut 8 squares, each 3½" x 3½".
	Dugout	1	3½"	Cut 8 squares, each 3½" x 3½".
Gold	Snowball	1	3½"	Cut 9 squares, each 3½" x 3½".
	Dugout	1	3½"	Cut 12 squares, each 3½" x 3½".
Green	Snowball	1	3½"	Cut 8 squares, each 3½" x 3½".
	Dugout	2	3½"	Cut 16 squares, each 3½" x 3½".
Turquoise	Rail	8	1½"	See * above.
	Hole in the Wall	2	3½"	Cut 48 rectangles, each 1½" x 3½".
	Hole in the Wall	4	1½"	See ** above.

Sewing

1. Referring to the quilt photo on page 94, "Rail Blocks" on page 57, "Dugout Blocks" on page 60, "Snowball Blocks" on page 60, "Hole in the Wall Blocks" on page 61, and the cutting chart, cut and assemble all required blocks. Group the blocks on a design wall.
2. Refer to "Assembling a Quilt Top with the Four-Patch Method" on page 62 to complete the quilt center.
3. Add the border, referring to the quilt photo and the cutting chart.
4. Refer to "Layering and Basting" on page 64 to prepare the quilt sandwich for quilting.
5. Quilt by hand or machine, as desired.
6. Refer to "Attaching the Binding" on page 65 and "Adding a Label" on page 66 to complete the quilt.

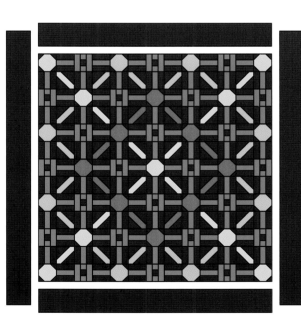

Bibliography

Brackman, Barbara, compiler. *Encyclopedia of Pieced Quilt Patterns.* Paducah, Ky.: American Quilters Society, 1993.

Cleland, Lee. *Quilting Makes the Quilt.* Bothell, Wash.: That Patchwork Place, 1990. Excellent resource for ideas on quilting your finished project.

Doak, Carol. *Your First Quilt Book (or it should be!).* Bothell, Wash: That Patchwork Place, 1990. Excellent book for beginning quilters.

Hanson, Joan, and Mary Hickey. *The Joy of Quilting.* Bothell, Wash.: That Patchwork Place, 1990. Excellent book for quilters of all levels; contains all the information that you need to piece, layer, quilt, and bind any quilting project.

Hopkins, Mary Ellen. *Baker's Dozen Doubled.* Santa Monica, Calif.: ME Publications, 1990.

____.*Connecting Up.* Santa Monica, Calif.: ME Publications, 1990. Source for the Four Patch Star design unit.

____.*The It's Okay If You Sit on My Quilt Book.* Santa Monica, Calif.: ME Publications, 1990. The original book that inspired the series of the same name.

Kimball, Jeana. *Loving Stitches.* Bothell, Wash.: That Patchwork Place, 1992.

Noble, Maurine. *Machine Quilting Made Easy.* Bothell, Wash.: That Patchwork Place, 1994.

About the Authors

Ann Castleberry was born in New Jersey and started sewing clothes for her family and friends when she was in the seventh grade. She continued to sew all her own and her mother's clothes until she discovered quilting in 1994. Since then, she has satisfied her urge to interact with fabric with quilting and now buys all her clothes. Her mother shops from catalogs. Ann's education and training is in analytical chemistry, and she does consulting work as an environmental chemist. Ann lives with her husband, Ed, son, Christopher, and three precocious Siamese cats in Gainesville, Florida, where she enjoys teaching at local quilt shops and guilds.

Mischele Hart was born in Florida. Her family traveled with the military until her father retired to Georgia. Mischele discovered sewing at an early age, but as a young mother, she became too busy chasing her sons and having fun to pursue creative sewing seriously. Her education and training are in nursing, and she worked as a nurse and volunteer until 1991, when she became co-owner of the Quilted Sampler shop in Tampa, Florida. Mischele is a popular quilting teacher and has taught in Florida and New England. She lives with her husband, Don, and has two grown sons, Brian and Leighton.